THANK YOU,

Georgette

...my 26 years in the Legislature

...when entering the Legislative halls, you leave the textbook behind, and democracy survives...

by Georgette B. Bérubé

authorHOUSE

1663 LIBERTY DRIVE, SUITE 200
BLOOMINGTON, INDIANA 47403
(800) 839-8640
WWW.AUTHORHOUSE.COM

© 2005 Georgette B. Bérubé. All Rights Reserved.

No part of this book may be reproduced, stored in a retrieval system, or transmitted by any means without the written permission of the author.

First published by AuthorHouse 12/16/04

ISBN: 1-4208-1770-1 (sc)
ISBN: 1-4208-1771-X (dj)

Library of Congress Control Number: 2004099701

Printed in the United States of America
Bloomington, Indiana

This book is printed on acid-free paper.

DEDICATION

To my constituents who allowed me to live this great experience…

> Bâtis ta citadelle loin de tous et très haut...
>
> Edmond Rostand, "La Citadelle"

TABLE OF CONTENTS

Name's Georgette 1

Remarks to Rotary International and Canadian Visitors 10/29/93 3

Growing Up In Lewiston 9

Political Campaigns
    The First Campaign 1970 17
    Congressional Campaign 1972 22
    Public Works Visit 1974 23
    Cohen Endorsement 26
    Run for Governor 1982 32
    State Senate Campaign 1984 35
    State Senate Campaign 1994 37
    Absentee Ballots 40

Issues And Programs
    Northern Ireland Divestiture 43
    South Africa Boycott 46
    Lewiston-Auburn Third Bridge 48
    Tobacco 'Sting' Program 51
    FAROG 52
    Petitions 57
    Studies 58

Partisanship / Personalities
    John L. Martin 65
    104th Birthday 69
    Democrat Yes, Republican No 70
    Worst Experience 71

Legislation
    Games of Chance 75
    Forum Francophone des Affaires 78
    Lewiston-Auburn College Start-up Funding 79
    Maine National Guard License Plates 80

GOVERNMENT
    State Auditor Election 85
    County Government 88

    Council on Aging *91*
    Quebec State Visit *93*
    A Farewell *95*

Pot Pourri
    Luncheon Canceled? *99*
    Polling *100*
    Sending Notes *101*
    Condoms Debated *103*
    Animals In Stores *104*

Random Thoughts
    Overview *109*
    Leadership *110*
    Follow the Leader *112*
    Term Limits *113*
    Spending / Taxes *115*

Remarks On Key Issues
    Power Authority Of Maine, 5/6/91 ....*119*
    Human Rights Bill (Gay Rights) 3/28/91 Senate Chamber *121*
    Abortion, House Chamber 5/19/71 .... *124*
    Equal Rights Amendment, House Chamber 2/27/73 .... *125*
    Democratic State Convention 1982 .... *127*

ACKNOWLEDGEMENTS

The word *gratitude* is too small indeed to express my appreciation for the support given me by my legislative colleagues during my tenure. I also received much assistance in book-writing from Natalie Dunlap and Donat Boisvert; advice from Tracey Mousseau who was instrumental in my being able to bring this project to fruition. I am grateful for the aid given by representative Kathleen Watson Goodwin (Ret.) who with Representative Lorraine Chonko (Ret.) so often inspired me against straying away from the Democratic Party, and to my children Michèle and Claude without whose support this manuscript could never have been written.

NAME'S GEORGETTE

The poet of the Senate, John W. Benoit from Rangely, announced that he was writing a poem about Senator Bérubé and that he would read it from the floor of the senate Chamber the night before adjournment:

NAME'S GEORGETTE by Senator John W. Benoit

She rode into town, it had been a long ride
"Name's Georgette," she said, "an' please step aside."

The crowd parted, at the hitching rail,
dismounting, her spur caught her horse's tail.

Not the best dismount she'd ever made,
as she rose from the dust and made for the shade.

"Name's Georgette," she said, "came to legislate,
hear the Senate bell ringing, so I guess I'm not late!"

She strode with class down the revisor's aisle,
"Name's Georgette," she said, "got some Bills to file."

The revisor stood, twin guns on her hips,
But a respectful smile was spread on her lips.

"Name's Georgette," she said, "ain't showin' no pity,
aim me in the direction of the Appropriations Committee!"

Other Senators cowered, and then stood aside,
Respecting the ordeal of this stranger's hard ride.

"Name's Georgette," she said, " this here Senate's been lax."
Been weeks in the sage, need to axe me a tax."

Then the Senate crowd muttered over one big thing,
Seems the local sheriff went by the name of King.

"Name's Georgette," she said, "these bills ought to pass,
right under the hammer, and please without sass."

Georgette B. Bérubé

Now the Senate President was a Lawrence named Mark,
Whose leadership style was more bite than mere bark.

But he held his tongue, fearing a long box of pine,
And told this stranger what she wanted was fine.

Well, one bill for fiscal soundness soon led to another,
And quickly the County's deficit lay in a smother.

"Name's Georgette," she said, "got no time for a fling,
need to talk fiscal sense to that sheriff named King."

Then the townsfolk made way, like herded cattle,
as she rode cross-town, tall in the saddle.

Who was that masked stranger? Buzzed around in the crowd.
Who was that masked stranger that made them all proud?

These several questions swirled in each person's noggin,
till one spoke: "She's the Lone Fiscal Ranger from Androscoggin!"

REMARKS TO ROTARY INTERNATIONAL AND CANADIAN VISITORS 10/29/93

There is a terrific musical trio here in Maine. They sing folk songs, talk of life in Maine, their name is SCHOONER FARE. Their latest CD has a song entitled QUEBECOIS...and it touches on names like Levesque, Corriveau... "They sweat all day from dawn till dusk, six days a week in the mills and shoe factories, it is work, it is family, it is church and God...a new life here and be who we are. But we'll go back home someday."

Just a song, but one that relates in a few words the pain and the struggles which these immigrants had to endure. A few did go back home but most stayed, made their mark, and now their children and grandchildren carry on their ideals, but in a more affluent lifestyle thanks to the hard work of their forebears.

The French presence has been felt in Maine ever since the 17th century after the French explorer Samuel de Champlain had made his first foray into North America in 1603 which was five years before he founded Québec City. He named this magnificent corner of America for a province in France, Le Maine, but it was not until the beginning of the 19th century that the first great migrations from French Canada started.

The Quebecers settled mostly in New England for different reasons than the Acadians who planted their roots in northern Maine in a beautiful land called the St. John Valley which borders New Brunswick. It was the period known as *"Le Grand Dérangement."* It was the expulsion in 1755 of these people of Nova Scotia by the British, an expulsion which would carry them as far as Louisiana...it was a very sad part of Canadian history.

Between the years 1871 and 1930 some 1.6 million Canadians came from Québec. And they chose to come for economic reasons though having been preceded in the late 1830s by others who were fugitives and exiles seeking safety from British prosecution for their part in the 1837 uprising in Québec. These economic reasons were due to the agricultural industry which had fallen into decline from the exhaustion of unfertilized fields, and the over-division of farms to provide lands for their too numerous sons. Thousands sought employment in the New England textile mills and shoe factories which hired whole families who worked from dawn till dusk and with wages of $6.00 for a week. These courageous and hopeful immigrants coming to a strange land, with a different language, did not undertake this dislocation because of political or religious reasons. It was the opposite of the reasons for the migrations from Europe: it was pure and simple necessity. Maine saw many arrive, and here in Lewiston they stepped down from the Canadian railroad trains at the Lincoln Street station, wide-eyed at the sight of giant mills...seeing themselves acquiring a richer and easier life than the one they were leaving. It was going to be only for a short time: go back home with enough money to buy land. They stayed...but at what price! These industrious and deeply religious people fed the labor-hungry factories, and they sacrificed with the near-loss of language and culture. It was quite a contrast with the serene pastoral life they had left behind. The mill owners liked these hardworking "canucks"...they also found them to be passive and docile.

When they came, they brought with them their clergy, founded their own churches with the apparatus for convents, schools, fraternal societies and importantly, a French press. Clergy were the elite, as were their doctors and religious teachers who followed. They lived in closely-knit homes and neighborhoods called Little Canada...they were a solid, active and respectful community. During World War I they enlisted, and they ran for political office. Their families grew: 10, 14, 19 children was not an unusual number but nevertheless they managed to save their money, later investing in tangible assets, something they could see and feel: land, real estate income, property. Their parish schools flourished, and for them, retention of the language was a primary need made more so by the drumming into them of the saying by the clergy: *"Qui perd sa langue perd sa foi."* (He who loses his language loses his Faith.) They would succeed in preserving both.

But that was a long time ago. What of today? What did they leave us that might have longtime impact on Lewiston, on Maine? In New England the contributions made by these French Canadians, now called Franco-Americans, were indeed many, and one of the most important was the legacy of a language. It is interesting to note that, of all the many ethnic groups to have settled here, French is the language that has continued to make its presence felt to a far larger degree than others. In an English-speaking milieu it was very easy to assimilate, and today it is even more difficult to retain one's language and ethnic culture. We live under the constant influence of English communications media. It was the language of work. Although the language of diplomacy remains French, finance and commerce are carried on in English. To some, the passage of years has caused them to regard their Gallic tongue as less of an insignia of honor, and to their children it often became an identification of inferiority because in order to survive they felt that they must conform, and without an accent betraying their roots.

There were no bankers as such among their group, yet banks hired them as tellers...after all, they had to attract the deposits of these thrifty workers who were rapidly accumulating savings. In turn, they became merchants, started banks, and even entered the world of politics. They became a political force, ran successfully for office...even their women... but that took longer. And some of the social world was closed to them and they could not easily access it; they could not at that time become members of the Rotary, for example.

A word that often creeps into books relating to French-Canadian immigrants is *survivance*. In my view, survival of any culture can be only maintained with its language, and it was the tenacity of our ancestors that kept it alive and helped maintain this *survivance*.

In our state French has no official status (such is not the case in Louisiana) and French Canadian history is relatively ignored and unknown in school textbooks, nonetheless, the language has remained alive. And if the young do not admit to wanting to learn it, their attitude changes once they reach adulthood. Populations have changed so that today in Lewiston, some 45 percent are still considered of French extraction, with about 30 percent knowing the language.

Aside from language as a great contribution in a multi-cultural society, there were many other contributions that stand as a tribute to the hard work and achievements of Franco-Americans. Certainly, staffing the mills and factories was instrumental to growth of Maine's economy and to the rest of New England, I might add. These good and upright citizens wrapped themselves in their family and church, which were central to their lives, and they left a legacy of values. The "Little Canadas" which were mentioned in passing were quiet, peaceful and spotless neighborhoods. Today most of the residents have moved to other parts of cities and little is left of their culture in those sections of Little Canadas.

But if they were faithful to work and religious beliefs, so too were they full of life enjoying music, dancing, plays, literature. There were serious writers living in Lewiston. There were musicians, and they patronized the theatre performing plays and operettas. Lewiston was once described by a Portland lawyer as a "cultural desert". Nothing could have been further from the truth. Performances at the Music Hall were always well attended, and to this day there is a diversity of cultural entertainment and the arts.

They also became members of the judicial department. Judge Armand Dufresne rose to become Chief Justice of the Maine Supreme Court and today we have some who sit on the District and Superior Courts.

They were successful businessmen and women: names like Marcotte, Benoit and so many others were respected merchants who contributed greatly in other ways such as the donating of funds to build the Marcotte Home. As sons and daughters became better educated, they in turn rose to be bank presidents, John Daigle to name one, Ronald Beauchesne another. The legal field abounds with attorneys of French-Canadian heritage.

Our largest building contracting firms are also Franco-American owned as are affiliated trades. The medical field has seen highly competent professionals who are surgeons and specialists who staff our hospitals. One such hospital, St. Mary's General Hospital, now called St. Mary's Medical Center, was founded by Canadian nuns who came here to tend the medical needs of their compatriots. They were competent, caring, dedicated, and they provided a great service to the entire area population.

Many of the older sons of these large families entered the priesthood, and to this day the Roman Catholic Diocese of Maine is staffed in great numbers by Franco-American clergy. Of the six Roman Catholic parishes in Lewiston, four were founded by the immigrants and are still called the French churches. And for the first time one of them was named as auxiliary Bishop of Maine, Bishop Proulx, followed by Auxiliary Bishop Cote.

We cannot forget education. Parochial schools were instrumental in educating the children and, although their numbers have diminished, today continue to be viable, and also to attract non-Catholic students. Teachers and administrators stressed discipline and they were devoted to their students. They imparted to them the work and study ethic thus better preparing them for entrance into the real world. Although many years ago the teaching nuns had classrooms of 40 students, there was never any disruption by the students. Perhaps sight of a leather strap hanging from the belt of a nun's habit was a deterrent to misbehaving. "Frenchies" also excelled in sports: baseball and boxing were two in which they became champs without forgetting hockey where they excelled. In politics, they made their mark and served honorably. I should not just say in the past tense…for they continue to do so as Mayors, City Councilors, and certainly in the State Legislature. French-Canadians as a collective group became a political force to contend with. Though fiscal conservatives generally, they are not insensitive to the social needs of their fellow-citizens. For the first time in Maine's history there have been two Francos who have been the presiding officers of the House of Representatives and Senate: House Speaker John L. Martin, who is proud to say that he is an Acadian, and Senate President Denis Dutremble who, by his middle of the road philosophy and approach to the Legislative process, coupled with his moderate views and instinct for conciliation, established pride and dignity in the Senate Chamber which has earned him the respect and trust from the opposition Party. And, yes, both Martin and Dutremble speak French.

The Franco-American voting block should not be taken lightly as it has been for too many years. Taken for granted, Lewiston often was left out when it came to appointments. Politically, Franco-Americans are centrists and tend to be more independent in their choices in the voting booth even straying away from their traditional Party ties. Such was the case in the Violette-Cohen race for Congress in 1972 and again for the 1978 U.S. Senate campaign.

All of these contributions have impacted our communities and all have been important in building solid foundations for our economic and intellectual well-being. This legacy is seen in a strong Roman Catholic Church and exemplified by the magnificent Saints Peter and Paul Church built by French-Canadian immigrants, paid for and built by them, even though money was scarce during the Great Depression. Their educational system is highly praised. All are a tribute and testimonial to their Faith and commitment to their hopes and aspirations.

Their struggle leading to achievements helped remove the stigmas and demeaning pejorative words like "Frog" and "Canuck" which were so inflammatory. Every so often, though, the stigma surfaces – maybe not in a deliberate manner, but because the idea of inferiority somehow lingers. An example: about ten years ago, a southern Maine newspaper carried an article referring to several major problems existing in the city of Biddeford, another city built by French-speaking Canadians, and it stated: "In the old days, of course, aside from a few sap buckets found attached to Central Maine Power utility poles during the maple syrup season each year, the City of Biddeford was pretty much a law and order kind of town." Unacceptable to say the least...

Through the years we have maintained close ties with families in Canada: Québec, New Brunswick, Nova Scotia...and while relatives disappear, cousins and friends remain, and we find that, as important as trade and government policies are to relationships between nations, the heart remains in the variety of contacts developed by the people among themselves. Our two societies have formed so many personal and institutional bonds over the years that it would be impossible to list them all. Many organizations such as the Rotary and Richelieu Clubs have chapters in both countries. This affiliation binds us. We see it so successfully with our tourism industry, on both sides of the border. In our State of Maine, in our immediate area, our strength is the diversity of culture; but the one unifying element is language, one which is shared with our neighbors to the North.

Georgette B. Bérubé

We are not immune to the problems of modern day living: issues of energy and environment, export and import of agricultural and wood products, fishing rights…all of these can be resolved if we sincerely keep open a line of communication made easier by our identity with other francophones using this French language as its intermediary.

The past is not a period to be relived, nor is it a time to be discarded lightly. We must heed with respect and wisdom, the soul of this heritage remaining conscious of the historical context which we share with our Anglophone fellow Americans. All of us must be fully committed to a two-fold mission: that of excelling within all cultures, and that of contributing to the ideal of national unity.

Merci à tous. Thank you all…

GROWING UP IN LEWISTON

In writing about issues and events that took place during my 26-year tenure in the Maine Legislature, I wondered what compelled me to initially seek office. What could I bring to the legislative process – what did I bring once elected?

I had never attended a Party caucus, in my case the Democrat Party; never spoken to or ever met the political leaders; yet, my interest in politics was deeply-rooted in that it was a subject often discussed at home; add to this a curiosity to see whether I could do better than who was representing my City at the time. My desire to run was certainly not motivated by a personal agenda. The only involvement my family had in politics was one of my father's older brothers who served two terms in the Canadian Parliament in Ottawa 1904 – 1908; of course, I had never met him. As to what could I bring? Well, if I ran and won, I would take with me the values learned from hard-working parents, emulate their moral code, spend within our means, help those less fortunate and always live what my father's favorite quote was: "observe the Golden Rule." What I did bring eventually to the policy-making process was steeped in familial values which shaped my political philosophy: government is there to help those who struggle to survive, to be prudent with taxpayers' money, to be fiscally responsible while remembering the needs of the disenfranchised.

"My uncle Aime Beauparlant who served in the Canadian Parliament.

Georgette B. Bérubé

Born in 1927 and brought up in the City of Lewiston, French was to me, as it was to many, the language of work, play, religion, and social functions. I spoke no English until I entered school, but once in kindergarten English took over. Total immersion, it seems, is the quickest way to learn a language and I did. Home was a safe haven with wonderful parents (Leonard and Blanche Beauparlant) who, though we lived through the Great Depression, nonetheless provided well for my brother Maurice and me: new clothing sometimes sewn from older ones, fresh cookies waiting for us at lunch and after school to where we walked in the morning, walk again home for lunch at noon, then again finally after school. There were no school buses in those days to carry us the ¾ mile distance each way. And then I remember my father who, after working from early morning to early evening came home and brought up wood from the cellar, climbing two flights of stairs with each armload so that the kitchen stove was always well-stocked and a warm, cozy place to dry up after our bath.

In those days, with little available cash, some parents made their children's toys. I remember a kite that my father had made for me after I had told him that I would like to send one soaring up into the sky. Out of a Kraft paper bag came a beautiful kite. The string had been saved by my mother from the wrapped meat bought at the neighborhood grocery store, the same one that sold the penny candy to the kids of the area. With the patience of Job, the owner would wait for the children to make their selection – all for a penny.

The Great Depression forced economies and I recall that during summer months there was an ice cream stand on the next street from where we lived and my mother would give me a nickel to buy an ice cream cone nearly every day. And friends and I would bicycle to get a taste of the wonderful Sawyer ice cream. One early evening, however, I lost my nickel on the way over and quickly returned home to ask for another one. My mother said she could not give me one, that a nickel was a lot of money and also that I had been inattentive having lost it and that I would have to wait until the next day for another one. This taught me a lesson for frugality and responsibility which I carried with me to the Legislature.

My father had a small furniture store on Lisbon Street. On Saturday afternoons the French-Canadian immigrants would use that day to shop, pay their bills and generally enjoy this day off from their tedious work, all dressed up in their Sunday best: ladies with hats and gloves, men in suit and tie. Often their day off ended with family gatherings with music and dancing. They found the energy to share dancing and laughter to the stringed fiddle reels on Saturday nights. While I did not grow up with the fiddling so well loved by these jovial and "I love life" people, Sunday evenings were devoted to piano and violin with my father joining the other violinist and friends and family members doing the piano accompaniment, while my mother always had an elaborate dinner ready for all of us.

"My father, Leonard Beauparlant, who built up his own business and taught himself how to play the violin."

As a child I often went with my father and watched him deal with customers and as I grew older I learned to appreciate these new citizens who also lived the work ethic brought from French-Canada. Business was conducted and closed with a handshake. That was the customer's promise to pay and the merchant's pledge to guarantee the purchase.

During the great shoe shop strike in the 1930s, I remember my father driving us by the factory gates one evening and I recall to this day the foreboding silence in the car. We communicated in hushed whispers if need be, and how frightened I was of the soldiers holding rifles as if a sound would activate those guns. My father told me that if people were not paid what they deserved to work and produce goods, they sometimes stopped working in order to impress upon the owner and bosses that without the workers they had no products to sell. So I learned about the working needs and the right to hold work stoppages. But I also learned from him that the owner must make enough profit to pay his workers.

I was taught that working at a job, any job, is not demeaning and if one is healthy, it is better to work for honest wages rather than wait for someone to give you money without earning it. "We must also live within our means," my father would say.

There is a French Canadian folk song entitled *"Les 100,000 façons de tuer un homme."* (The 100,000 ways of killing a man.) It says that you can kill a man by giving him a gun and sending him to war, he can be killed by the guillotine, etc., but the worst way of killing a man is to pay him to do nothing, for that creates a city of walking dead.

And so, after working in and later co-managing my father's store with my brother for over twenty years, I brought the business principles coupled with compassion toward the needy to the Legislature. My parents' espousal of hard work plus living within our means readied us for the adult world. My fiscal conservatism was fostered by my upbringing. But I was always reminded that we must lend a helping hand to the less fortunate.

"With my mother."

While I learned these values from my parents, along the way I encountered strict discipline (of which I did not have too much while growing up) from the nuns both at parochial school and at the girls' boarding school I attended. The teaching Order of Dominicans in Sabattus, Maine strove to instill the work ethic, discipline and to force me to eat food that I did not like (to this day, over six decades later, I do not eat peanut butter and jelly sandwiches.)

One event truly propelled my trip to the Maine Legislature and that was during an evening at home. My husband, Gerry, was also Franco-

American. He was raised in Auburn, Maine and was among the first students to attend the new St. Dominic High School founded by Fr. François Drouin, a highly respected Dominican priest. Like most men of my generation, Gerry was drafted into military service during World War II. He had just turned 18 and was just a few months from graduating from St. Dominic High School. By August 1944 he was fighting in France with General Patton's Third Army against the German Army and the severe frostbite suffered during the Battle of the Bulge ended his combat. He spent the next several months recuperating at a Luxembourg Palace, which had been converted to a U.S. Army hospital. He returned after the war and worked in the community. We were married by Fr. Drouin in January 1952 and had two children. Early in 1970 I suppose I had begun complaining about politicians because one night after work, Gerry put his Lewiston Evening Journal down, took a sip from his martini, and told me "put your money where your mouth is. Better yet, put my money where your mouth is. Let's go run a campaign." Gerry never had a desire to participate in politics but he made friends easily, and simply because I expressed a thought he was ready to help me in this endeavor.

Preparation for elective office can come from textbooks or just plain common sense. I'll subscribe to the common sense approach for it mirrors more accurately the feelings of those we are elected to serve. Armed with the will to achieve the objective which I had set for myself, that of truly being a representative of the people, I embarked on an exciting trip.

When it was done, I was the longest-serving woman to serve in Maine Legislative history; only three men (John Martin and Louie Jalbert included) served longer.

And now, having finally retired, never to return to public office, I decided to put my thoughts and experiences on paper in the hope that it will lend some understanding to state politics and policies between 1970 and 2000. I think it also important to recount what happened behind the scenes of legislation - the scenes which are otherwise unrecorded in the Legislative Record - and how decisions on bills really happen in a state government which is an often overlooked segment of our system.

These pages will give the reader a glimpse into what sometimes transpires in dealing with legislation. I begin this work with words from a speech that I gave several years ago to visiting Canadians of the Rotary International, the reason being that it will give a better idea of how I was influenced by my upbringing in a Franco-American environment and how it affected my political philosophy.

POLITICAL CAMPAIGNS

"Our family photo for the first newspaper ad in my campaign."

THE FIRST CAMPAIGN 1970

Saturday, 8:20 am, February 1970. I picked up the old ringing rotary phone and after the customary "Hello" a man's gruff voice said:

"This is Louis."

"Louis?" I asked.

"Louis Jalbert," came the imperious reply. He continued:

"I hear that you're thinking of running for the House [of Representatives]. I can tell you right now that you're not going to win. Now, if you're interested in politics, you should start by joining the County Democratic Women's Club. They're getting ready for a card party as a fund-raiser. You can help them set up the tables. That's where you start."

Little did he know that this was not what I had in mind. I subscribed to the saying: "Make policy, not coffee." After recovering from the initial shock I responded:

"How can you say this…you don't even know me nor what I am capable of in serving in the Legislature…"

But before I could continue, he interrupted: "My dear, I know everything about you, including the size of your underwear."

I was stunned! Stunned at the insolence, particularly coming from the mouth of the so-called leader of the Democrat Party. He then went on to explain, spelling out in graphic language, how "they" would defeat me in the primary election. Thus was I introduced to "Mr. Democrat" and to the world of politics.

Mr. Jalbert, or "Mr. D" as he liked to be called, had shown absolutely no interest in my views on issues so vital to the people of our city and state. Yet, his attitude told me that his only concern was to ensure that the power to control not be eroded from his hands by someone with a mind of their own, if by a fluke she were elected. I say "she" because there had never been a woman elected to the House from Lewiston. My city's Democratic Party leaders were a male-dominated "good old boy" club who followed orders. And I was subsequently told by a local member of "that" club, "what would a woman know about politics." The ideals and goals that I cherished were suddenly shattered: nonetheless, they would guide me in my decision to seek office. In doing so, I would discover that while there are those who, to seek control, misuse power; many more exist who are genuinely dedicated to easing the burdens of daily life for their fellow citizens – Louis Jalbert was not one of the latter.

After hanging up on me, my antagonist then called my husband at work and advised him to "keep the little woman at home to take care of the kiddies." Gerry was principled and had a strength of character which he gained from his family and experience in the war. He did not back down when doing what was right was at issue. The caller was told in no uncertain terms that my family was supportive of my endeavor. Threats which initially were dismissed were to be proven prophetic in a few short years when "Mr. D" had the Administrator of the hospital fire Gerry, a decision which was shortly thereafter rescinded because of the support the hospital staff gave to my husband.

Perhaps my mother was correct when she said to me after I had called to tell her of my interest in seeking elective office, "but why would you want to do that…they're not honest people." Heeding her advice might have saved me the aggravation stemming from the "take no prisoners" attitude of Party loyalists. I was considered an intruder. But had I caved in, decided not to run, I would have been deprived of participation in a great adventure, working in the greatest democratic system in the world, and I would have missed the chance of making a positive impact on peoples' lives. It was bad enough that I had not sought permission to run, but worse, I was a woman perceived as wanting to usurp what up to that time had been a safe, secure male domain.

Textbooks do not teach what to expect in political campaigns. I found it offensive that instead of discussing issues that might separate us, tactics used by Party "hacks" centered on removal of lawn signs, character assassination and threats to supporters.

With regard to lawn signs I was fortunate that my husband, brother and friends would immediately replace them as fast as they were broken or taken away outright. One of my supporters called to tell me that the sign they had put up on their lawn had been taken. This was only one of many calls I received. They told me that shortly after dusk a car would pull up in front of their house, remove my campaign sign, and place it in their trunk. My husband and brother took my brother's car and waited across the street from one of the homes. Surely enough, after dark a car pulled up, two men removed the sign and put it in their trunk. There was little my husband and brother could do – painted on the car was the word "Sheriff."

More frustrating was the pressure brought to businesses that had placed my posters in their shop windows or within their establishments. In one instance, this coercion occurred when a bar restaurant owner placed a VOTE FOR GEORGETTE sign over the bar. The next day I received his frantic call…he had been told to remove "that broad's sign" or he might lose his liquor license. I suggested that he take it down, but I also reminded him that he would be voting in the secrecy of the voting booth. The secret ballot…what a godsend. Throughout that campaign and subsequent ones I would constantly stress that point.

Thank You, Georgette

Many overzealous campaign workers disregarded the protocol and in some cases the voters would be asked to sign several application forms which were then held until the next election, at which time a ballot would be picked up and brought to the voter, even though by that time he or she might be unable to physically vote. Easy to see how there could be fraud.

During that first campaign, I received a call from a man who said that his father had just voted by absentee ballot at Lewiston's largest nursing home. He questioned this since his father had been a "vegetable" for over one year. It was no exaggeration when, in a Party caucus, "Mr. D" pridefully stated that "when the polls open on election day, I have 250 votes in my pocket," which roughly corresponded to the number of nursing home residents. I promised myself that if elected, I would introduce legislation to curb this abuse.

In the year 1970, selection of nominees in the Primary election was by an at-large voting district meaning that the entire city voters selected their Party's nominee, as opposed to the current single-member district where the City is divided in districts and the voters select a candidate for their district only. Based on population, Lewiston was entitled to six House seats, with the six top vote getters of each political party in the primary to face each other in the November general election. That year saw fourteen Democrat candidates vying for the six seats, most having been selected by the Party machine. Surprisingly I placed third, thereby assuring myself a place on the Fall ballot.

On the evening of that November election, friends and supporters dropped by our home to wish me well. Election results had not as yet been tabulated, fueling some nervousness on my part at least. My thoughts went back to the campaign. "Good luck, Mrs. Bérubé," "We need you up there in Augusta." Those words were also a reminder that with winning comes responsibility, for people place their trust in their elected officials and that belief should not be betrayed. All we citizens ask is that you be honest with them, and make them proud that you serve them. Once having gained their approval, it is incumbent upon all those who serve the public to place personal agendas aside and partisan politics second to the peoples' wishes. It was that philosophy that led me not to oppose – as other legislators did - the results of a term limit referendum supported by Maine residents which led me to depart the State Senate in 1996.

I was also remembering that first outing at campaigning. It was eleven o'clock in the evening at the changing of shifts at Bates Mill, when there were still three shifts, or indeed any. Hundreds of people streamed in and out of these vast forbidding brick buildings. As I opened the car door to begin my walk toward the mill gate (it felt more as though I was walking the plank), I suddenly developed stage fright and did not move. Would I be rebuffed? After a gentle shove by my husband, who was also my chauffeur, I approached a man who was slowly walking toward his workplace, smoking a corncob pipe, swinging a black lunch pail. How many hundreds – no, thousands – had trudged these same worn sidewalks for little pay, few benefits, yet giving their all.

I handed him a campaign bookmatch and said that I would need his vote. Stopping to read the message on the cardboard ad, he took a puff from his pipe, looked up at me and said in French: "*Une femme? Pourquoi pas.*" (A woman? Why not.) He then continued his slow pace to his all-night job…I thought that if I made it, my decisions would affect him and so many like him…what an awesome responsibility. I promised myself that I would not be a disappointment to him nor to so many like him… "A woman? Why not!" became my campaign slogan.

My husband was now at my side having parked the car, and his presence gave me encouragement. One man stopped and said as I met him and others walking with him, "never forget the working man, the one who works all the time. Don't take all of his earned money, but when a catastrophe hits him such as losing his job, be there to help him through a difficult time."

I remember vividly that first foray into campaigning. None of us – family, friends – had ever campaigned. Needless to say, we were apprehensive.

My spirits buoyed by the encouraging comments which met me during this first campaign, I and my family charged into an uncharted political process with vigor and determination. It wasn't so bad after all; in fact, it was downright fun. However, had it not been for the gracious words of support from voters, I might not have continued.

Having made it through the Primary, my election in November was nearly assured as no Republican generally gained a seat – not since the mid 20th century. But having been victorious, I also attracted the wrath of those who had predicted my demise. "We'll defeat you with all the ammunition we have." This now rang hollow on the evening of the November election, particularly as the returns came in. The greatest pleasure on that November night came when I led the winners having bested five other names on the ballot under the Democrat column for I had received 12,133 votes, and Mr. Jalbert garnered 12,132 votes.

"Should we ask for a recount?" asked my husband with tongue in cheek.

As all of us unwound after the final results were announced, again I thought of the many people whom I had met at the factory gates, at their places of business, the elderly – all had entrusted me with their future. I prayed that I would never let them down and that I would represent them with the dignity they all deserved. I vowed never to benefit financially from my service and I did not – I still buy solid, used cars and I still live in the same house my husband and I bought 48 years ago. Nor would I forget my husband's only advice: "Remember that you'll get old someday, and never, never forget the military veteran."

A family friend and advisor said to me as he was leaving our home that exciting evening: "Remember this victory…there will never be another one like it." He was right.

And so, that evening of Tuesday, November 3, 1970, saw the culmination of a hectic campaign. The "Thank You" newspaper ad which I ran the next morning simply said:

<blockquote>PEOPLE OF LEWISTON, I LOVE YOU.
GEORGETTE</blockquote>

The morning after our sweet victory, Lewiston was greeted by lawn signs which, as if by magic, had sprouted cardboard banners with the words: **Thank You (signed Georgette)**. My husband had stapled those thank you signs till the early morning hours…the election triumph was due in great part to him.

CONGRESSIONAL CAMPAIGN 1972

In 1972, a young mayor from Bangor, an unknown Republican to most in central Maine, came campaigning in Lewiston as the Republican nominee for Congress; he would later become a Secretary of Defense. He worked extremely hard while running against a man whom I thoroughly respected, having served with him in the State Legislature. Democratic State Senator Elmer Violette from Van Buren was a Franco-American of Acadian descent, with deep convictions and integrity who was expected to win hands down, counting heavily on the French-speaking Democrats of Lewiston who voted in large numbers, thus ensuring him a win. Candidate Cohen had picked up on the 'take them for granted Francos' and he paid special attention to the citizens of this ethnic group. At that first election of his many to come, he had not carried the city that was so predominantly Democrat, but he had succeeded in making inroads eroding the Democrat support and establishing his credibility.

That fall, I was privileged to campaign, as a volunteer, with Senator Violette, climbing flights of stairs in tenement buildings with him, to visit workers on night shifts, hosting receptions in my home. Unknown to me at that time was the lukewarm support for his candidacy by the local political machine. On the night of the election I received a phone call from John Martin who wanted to know how the vote count was going in Lewiston saying: "I can trust you to level with me."

After giving him the latest tally which clearly indicated that Violette had a comfortable lead, John said: "It isn't enough, Georgette, he should have done better there. We were done in by some members of our own Party." Indeed candidate Cohen had eaten into the Democrat stronghold and he became the new Congressman for Maine .

PUBLIC WORKS VISIT 1974

The 1974 gubernatorial election was one of the most interesting statewide races I ever witnessed. The Democratic nominee was George Mitchell who had worked as an aide to Senator Ed Muskie. The Republican nominee was Linwood Palmer, the House Republican Leader. The third candidate was an Independent from Lewiston, James Longley. One day, Jim walked into the store during his campaign route. I didn't think he had a chance. He looked at me and said: "I'm going to win, Georgette." His confidence convinced me that I was wrong, that the major parties were underestimating him and Lewiston.

During my political campaigns, as was my custom, I visited the employees as they arrived in the yard of the Lewiston Public Works where I had always been well received. On this November 1974 morning at 6:15am to be exact, I stood outside the main entrance talking to the men as they entered the building to get their day's assignment. I knew many of them and they chatted with me. A short time after I had arrived, Democratic gubernatorial candidate George Mitchell walked up the drive accompanied by his County campaign coordinator and two County officials. I knew George Mitchell to be an intellectual, a hard worker, honest and a gentleman. He shook my hand, wished me luck and I did the same. As he entered the building, the County political activist said to me: "This is George's morning. What are you doing here?"

"The same thing Mr. Mitchell is doing," I replied.

The Androscoggin County Party machine could never accept that I did not ask their permission on how and when to campaign, and also that I received more votes than their candidates. Never was I asked to assist other Democrat candidates in their quest for elective office.

While Mr. Mitchell and the hangers-on stayed in the building, I remained outdoors and continued to greet people by that cool early November day. Within a few minutes, the union steward came outside and very politely said to me in subdued tone:

"Mrs. Bérubé, maybe you should leave. Some of those accompanying Mitchell feel that you're taking attention away from his visit."

"But I've always visited here since my first campaign," I said, to which he added sheepishly, "I'm very sorry, but I've been asked to do this."

"Okay…but that's another reason why Jim Longley will be elected Governor. Just keep it up."

I was on the brink of tears and as I started to leave, he said to me, "Thanks for making it easy for me. You are a gracious lady."

Georgette B. Bérubé

I went directly to work where I related the story to my brother who also worked at the family business. During that forenoon he went to the restaurant next door to pick up a coffee. It was also the mid-morning coffee stop for many Public Works employees. It was a place where patrons and owners talked baseball, hockey (Lewiston had a minor league team at the time), football and politics. My brother mentioned the episode of earlier that morning. Shortly thereafter, a City truck driver came through the front door asking, "Is it true?"

"Yes," I said.

"We'll see about that," as he left still sputtering.

Close to noontime, to my great surprise, George Mitchell walked into the store with hand extended.

"Georgette, I want you to know that I had nothing to do with what happened earlier and I want to apologize for that."

I assured him that he bore no blame and I would continue to support him. But I also cautioned him that perhaps he should distance himself from a Party machine which did more harm than good.

He was not to be the victor this time. The mood of the citizens was for change and a new face had surfaced in the run for the governorship, a new face indeed that did not spout the same rhetoric that politicians repeat *ad nauseum*. They saw that change in James Longley who would become Maine's Independent Governor.

The future governor Jim Longley had dropped by on his walk through Lewiston's Lisbon Street. What struck me was his certainty of a victory accentuated by his piercing azure blue eyes, a look reminiscent of the brilliant 'see through you' gaze of the late TV. host, Bishop Fulton J. Sheen. If his confidence had not impressed me, his eyes clearly had its effect if perhaps momentarily, and I too became convinced of the possibility of his success.

George Mitchell possessed the intellectual ability to serve with greatness as he subsequently proved when he was appointed to fill the unexpired U.S. Senate term of Senator Edmund Muskie in 1980 who had been appointed this country's Secretary of State. George Mitchell certainly became more partisan and supported many of the more liberal wing's positions as he quickly ascended in the Senate, but I believe that was due more to his position as Senate Majority Leader. Despite his partisanship, I always believed he would have made a good, honest, committed and ethical President of the United States. I continue to believe that as of this writing in 2002.

Thank You, Georgette

"With then-Senator Ed Muskie. He later served as the Secretary of State under President Jimmy Carter. His protégé, George Mitchell, served out his term in the Senate and distinguished himself as a leader."

COHEN ENDORSEMENT

For a time I had felt that my Party, the Party of Roosevelt, Truman, Kennedy, was bent on a more liberal course than the majority of enrolled Democrats wanted. Party caucuses and conventions became dominated by a vocal liberal minority whose philosophy was alien to the more moderate and fiscally conservative views of the people of my District. The overwhelming Democrat vote was taken for granted with little attention given to the city. To rectify this, I firmly believed that change must come from within.

And so, after much thought and knowing full well the political ramifications which my action would engender, on September 8, 1977 I announced at a press conference held in my home that I had sent a letter to Congressman Cohen urging him to seriously consider seeking the U.S. Senate seat the following year, a seat held by Senator William Hathaway. I did not want to cast aspersions on the Senator, but I felt that his ultra liberal voting record was not reflective of the views held by the Franco-American community and that Congressman Cohen had a more traditional approach more in tune with the citizens of my community. My letter read:

Dear Congressman Cohen:

From all accounts in the press it would appear that you have not arrived at a final decision on whether to seek the Governorship of our State or the U.S. Senate seat. As our Congressman, you have remembered the voters of my City of Lewiston as no other U.S. Representative has. During your first campaign I recall you said that when you were elected you would open an office locally in order to better serve us and in turn have input from the citizens of this community...this you did after holding your victorious press conference here the day following the election thereby acknowledging the importance you attached to our people. Your willingness to listen to our views on many issues, irrespective of Party affiliation, explains your victories.

Your views parallel my own philosophy and are reflective, I feel, of that of many of my fellow citizens of Lewiston...the very same people who value integrity and honesty in government, and individualism above partisan politics.

During the next crucial six years, major decisions will be made by our Senator: decisions involving national defense and security, energy, safeguarding private enterprise in productive employment while remembering the duties and privileges associated with all of our rights… these decisions will demand that we be given a choice of selecting a person who reflects the moderate hinking of so many people of my community and my State. From your years of proven service and experience for us in Washington, I feel that you are the person to do this…and so, although perhaps forward on my part, I nevertheless ask that you actively seek the Office of U.S. Senator. I stand ready to support you.

Sincerely,
Georgette B Bérubé

This announcement generated sometimes vitriolic comments from the local Party activists, which was expected. But the many positive comments wiped out the less than supportive ones. During the next few days I was comforted by the support and encouragement expressed by the people of my City. Of all the letters and notes I received only three (two unsigned) chastised me for "daring to come out for a Republican." One of the unsigned letters bordered on the humorous. It came from the Androscoggin Democrat Women's Club (the "card-party group" that Louis Jalbert once suggested that I join instead of running for office), typed on onion paper, advising me that I and another Cohen supporter who was a heavy contributor to the Democrat Party were being expelled from their group. No signature. Queried by the press for my reaction I said: "I feel as though I've been sent to the Gulag Archipelago."

My dues check of $2 was returned. So much indignation by some of the very people who had concealed their lack of support for their own 1972 congressional candidate!

A Democrat legislator called on Speaker Martin to remove me as chair of the Audit and Program Review Committee. The crime? Endorsing a Republican! So much for freedom of thought. An editorial in the Lewiston Daily Sun read:

Representative Bérubé is not the first nor will she be the last to endorse a candidate of the opposing Party. The old politics called for such endorsements to be made in the backroom away from the public view. Mrs. Bérubé took no such route. She announced her support for Representative Cohen publicly. Actually, her "political sin" is not so much that she supports an opposition candidate, it is because she "went public." Still it is refreshing to have someone in politics take an action considered right, even though it could have embarrassing consequences. It will be interesting to see if our Lewiston lawmaker retains her chairmanship when the Legislature reconvenes in January.

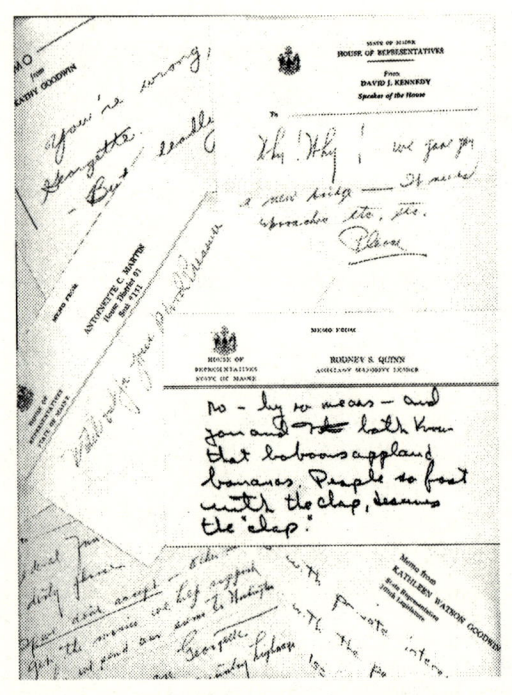

"Although I took heat from my own party for supporting Republican Bill Cohen, my decision proved right as he went on to serve in the Senate, took some difficult stands himself, and also served as Secretary of Defense – ironically in an Administration of the same party as that which took issue with my original support."

In 1979 a Democrat activist from Livermore Falls, Joseph Langlais, wrote to long-time Party insider Harold Pachios, a fair man, saying:

During the last year I've heard you say a number of times that the Party system is in trouble, the voters are shying away from Party politics and registering as Independents. I'd like to know why and what to do about it. Now here is a good reason: Georgette Bérubé was the first politician to come through for Bill Cohen, before he even announced. At the time, when we asked why this woman was tolerated as a Democrat, your answer was: 'Everyone is entitled to a difference of opinion and we don't bounce anyone out of the Party because of it, or just because they don't agree with us.' Now, my friend, we find this woman is complimented with a co-chair on what some people consider an important committee. The question at this time, though we do not take action against a difference of opinion is it necessary to reward them for it? I think that there are many other Democrats more deserving: if not, then I would rather see a Republican in that position than Mrs. Bérubé. This is the kind of action that makes people say: 'Politicians are all alike, put them in a bag and shake it and they all come out the same color regardless of their label.' It was these so-called Democrats who supported Bill Cohen that sparked the anti-Hathaway vote in November and the Party is that much poorer because of it.

A response came from John Martin:

Dear Mr. Langlais:

I have received the copy of your letter to Hal Pachios regarding the appointment of Rep. Georgette Bérubé as House chairman of the Joint Standing Committee on Audit and Program Review. I realize that such an action may be difficult to understand to those who may not have all the facts. Although Rep. Bérubé had been the top vote-getter in Lewiston for some time, Bill Hathaway had never once contacted her until she announced for Cohen. Only after her endorsement of Cohen did he finally bother to call her. Perhaps this was because of the various factions in Lewiston. Cohen had also voiced strong support for the interest of Franco-Americans which Bill had never done. Rep. Bérubé is a conservative Democrat who was never at ease with Bill's more liberal philosophy. Also she was offered a staff position with Cohen but refused. While I do not approve of her endorsement of Cohen, at least she had the honesty to do it openly before the Primary instead of after she was home free.

Further alienating her from the Party would serve little purpose, since she is popular with her constituents and may be of assistance to the Democratic candidates in the future. As Treasurer of Elmer Violette's congressional campaign I can attest to her strong support while many others sat on their hands.

I am sure this response will not satisfy you completely, but I hope it will help you to better understand my decision.

Pressure had been applied with John to remove me as chair, and to a legislator he responded, "while I do not approve of her decision, she is able and competent and she stays." John Martin, as the Speaker of the

House and one of the leading Democrats in the state had every right and opportunity to remove me from the chairmanship. That he did not seek retribution bespeaks volumes of the side of him that I got to know but that the public, especially the media, rarely saw. In the twenty-six years we served together at the Capitol, John and I agreed on some issues and disagreed on others, but we were always straight with each other. I never forgot the fairness he showed during this especially trying time.

My announcement was made some seven months before the next Primary election and it was obvious that candidates would be found to run against me. Since the next election would be from the new single member districts, the feeling was that I could be easily defeated. On the issue of single member districts, while the machine did not support it, I had voted for this change as I believed that the elected officials from the new districts would be more responsive and accountable to their constituents as they would be the sole representative from a particular area thereby demanding accountability on their part instead of riding the coattails of others.

In announcing for Bill Cohen months ahead of the Primary, I risked much, but I chose to do so before the next Primary election thus allowing voters to be the judge. A candidate, Gerald Bouffard, was indeed found to oppose me and he was billed as "The Real Democrat." My faith in the fairness of the electorate was again rewarded when I was re-nominated in June 1978. The vote tally:

BÉRUBÉ	1,218
BOUFFARD	384

He had even lost his own precinct.

After reconvening in January 1979, during one of our Democrat caucuses a then flaming young liberal (who later changed to the Republican Party, to the far right of the Republican Party, I might add) suggested to the members that I should leave the Democratic Party.

I sent a note to the Assistant Majority Leader Rodney Quinn, a veteran World War II bomber pilot who would later become Maine's Secretary of State. My note said that I would be glad to oblige if he wanted me to do so. His response: "NO. By no means – and you and I both know that baboons applaud bananas. People so fast with the clap, deserve the 'clap' and that's reason they need people like you and me to give some balance and directions."

Thank You, Georgette

"Jim Longley. An Independent who overcame the odds against two established parties to win a term as Governor."]

RUN FOR GOVERNOR 1982

With little money and no paid staff, I embarked in 1982 on a campaign to wrest the democratic nomination from the incumbency in the Governor's chair.

The tidy sum of $14,000 is what we had to press on to a Primary contest. The meager dollars had mostly been contributed by non-political citizens from all walks of life. But I had a resource that money could not buy: loyal friends and loving family. Those were my assets and they would be pitted against the over $200,000 being spent by my opponent in that June election. It would be an impossible task to unseat a sitting Governor. Nonetheless, I accepted the challenge.

Advisors suggested and indeed encouraged me to by – pass the Primary by running as an Independent, thus making it easier to achieve our goal. It was logical that skipping a costly Primary battle would give me more time to get my name known throughout this vast State of Maine. My strategy was not so much a run against the Governor but rather to stick to positive programs and issues, as well as placing my candidacy as an alternative. The great fear, however, was that I could very well be throwing the race to the Republicans. There was also the question: do it as an Independent or wait for 1986?

For a long time I had witnessed changes in my Party. Some of the changes were from the ultra-liberal left-wing of the Party and not representative of the rank and file, changes in philosophy, changes in growth of government. Extend these changes and 'new' directions to the left of the Party platform, proposed legislation, all told me that the new faces were not about to accommodate the more traditional centrists of our Party. I believed that there must be some place in the whole legislative agenda for the majority of Mainers who believed in helping those who truly need assistance and those who only ask that their tax dollars be used effectively to alleviate poverty and environmental problems, to enforce fair labor laws and to ensure that the needed tools for educating our young people be provided to teachers. I also believed that change must come from within. So, as I traversed this wonderful state, I discovered how vast it is. From Kittery to Fort Kent I saw the differences in topography and people. The warmth of the north country people in Aroostook County, with its pastoral serenity, differs from the more heavily populated industrialized south, but everywhere I was received with great courtesy which included encouraging words. It was a great experience.

I must say that the campaign waged by my opponent, Mr. Brennan, was positive in that there were none of the negative shots that we all have been

Thank You, Georgette

subjected to in recent years. In fact, he and his troops pretended that I did not exist. Although in the only televised debate he consented to on WGAN television, many said that I had bested the Governor. The cameraman said, "Right on. You were tops."

All in all it was a pleasant experience, albeit some tactics were not worthy of the Governor. For instance, two of my supporters in York County told me that they could no longer support my candidacy as "Joe" had appointed them to some boards. I do not believe that Governor Brennan had thought of that, but too often loyalists in a political camp take license by stooping to these tactics.

"Speaking with Governor Joseph Brennan"

The State Party convention brings out, along with agendas, platforms and slapping of shoulders doing so with the enthusiasm that members hope will ignite their troops and carry them to success at election time. We cannot forget to mention that a convention is enlivened by the loud demonstrations as they parade around the convention hall to fast loud music. While my troops were few in number, I felt good seeing this ragtag bunch of supporters, with hats and horns, marching past the platform stage: a handful making as much noise and hoop-la as the well-oiled and well-organized Brennan demonstrations.

The tally on election day was not good for me. With Primary elections notorious for low voter turnout, the odds were not favorable. Since there wasn't much money there were few advertisements. But one popular giveaway was fortune cookies with the inside message plugging my candidacy. The idea was not mine but came from my son who was then a teenager.

Georgette B. Bérubé

Claude has eagerly campaigned with me starting out as a 4 year-old boy. Standing by my side at mill gates, he handed out brochures with a winning smile. When he grew older, he ran for the Student Senate and achieved his first victory. This first victory was due in part to his creative ability such as the fortune cookies, which he thought was a good idea.

Arriving early at school the morning of the election he passed them out to each student. In each cookie was a message reading "Claude Bérubé for Student Senate." How had he gotten the idea? From one of his National Geographic magazines in which was a recipe on how to bake fortune cookies. Not an easy thing to do in a small oven. Once baked, these egg white concoctions must be folded quickly before they harden up, and the paper message must be inserted. It takes a long time to bake a batch and while I made the cookies, Claude was typing out his ad. He won. And so I had some fortune cookies made for this campaign but, while they were attention getters, I still lost.

STATE SENATE CAMPAIGN 1984

In 1984 after a two-year hiatus from the Legislature and weighing my chances of winning the State Senate seat from eight-term Senator Carroll Minkowsky, I decided to seek this office and continue to represent this district. Some pundits (from my own Party I might add) predicted that I could never take Mr. Minkowsky, or that at best it would be a very close election with the same outcome. Some still resented my having supported now Senator William Cohen while conveniently forgetting that my voting record was far more liberal than my opponent's, as well as nearer to the Democratic philosophy than his was at the time. While Senate district 16 included most of the city of Lewiston, eight towns also were part of the district: Sabattus, Greene, Turner, Leeds, Minot, Lisbon, Wales and Livermore.

Many things affect peoples' perception of a candidate. Issues of course are foremost but also is the image which a candidate projects. In his campaign announcement, Minkowsky was quoted as saying: "There's no doubt about it. I'm fiercely independent, bold and not a traditional Democrat who finds it difficult to accept change." Our views were similar on some issues, for I, like him, was a fiscal conservative always seeking accountability for how monies were spent and for what purpose. However, we differed on social needs and human rights issues. As an example of my opponent's thinking, he said on the Senate floor (reprinted verbatim) in voting on the Human Rights Bill, that he was "voting against, not because I have any hang-ups. It's based on my own Christian faith taught to believe not a proper life style. I've got friends who are gay, lesbians and they're not enchanted at having a statutory law that will change their particular posture in life. It's not in the best interest of society; our purpose in life basically is to love and respect our fellow man and woman and to fulfill one of the objects of life of reproducing our own kind."

Statements like these do not ingratiate you with the electorate.

Another example where he straddled the line on both sides: on a crucial vote on a pro-labor workers' compensation bill, he stated, again on the floor of the Senate: "The public is not fully aware of the ramifications of what this is all about. I'm against this bill, but will vote for it." On increasing minimum wages: "Not less of a Democrat for voting against this bill, my concerns as a Democrat are for small business. I have agonized. I want the record to show very clearly that I am compassionate and very much in tune with the needs of those who work for minimum wages, but this afternoon I will have to vote against this particular issue." Comments such as these did not please many of the voters and no doubt contributed to his defeat.

One of his votes was key to legislation that created the state income tax. Initially pegged at 4% it has grown to 8%. Mr. Minkowsky, who had voted against it initially, switched his vote and thus cast the one decisive vote to enact the income tax law.

The Primary elections are often difficult because candidates are trying to best a member of the same political Party. I was elated at the outcome:

                Bérubé   1115
                Minkowsky 598

STATE SENATE CAMPAIGN 1994

Every ten years there is a redistricting of Senate and House districts based on the most recent census of the population. It is the Legislature's prerogative to draw the lines and it is generally conceded that the Party in control drafts those lines to the benefit of that Party. But when there is disagreement, the decision is left up to the State Supreme Court, which is what happened in 1993.

The City Clerk of Lewiston, Gerald Bérubé (one of my husband's many cousins), disagreed with the Legislature's proposed new district for Senate districts 16 and 23 which were held by myself and Democrat Senator James Handy. The City official had drawn his own lines placing Mr. Handy and myself in the same district, which would cause us to run against one another in the Primary if we chose to seek re-election in the following Primary. Even after we enlisted the support of the chair of the Redistricting Commission, Senator Richard Carey of Waterville, try as we might, the City Clerk was adamant. We never quite figured out his reasons but as a result the controversy was sent to the Court who accepted his suggestion.

This was not an election battle that I looked forward to. Some liberal Senators tried to dissuade me from running. Added to that was the availability of union money for Senator Handy and that gave me concern. Nonetheless, I announced my intention to seek re-election to the new District 21.

I accepted an invitation to appear before the local teachers' union committee that was interviewing candidates. It was obvious that they would support my opponent disregarding my excellent record on education issues. A letter was sent to the teachers requesting that they support Mr. Handy, and I received a letter from the President of the Maine Education Association explaining their reason for endorsing Handy. It read:

Dear Senator Bérubé:

On behalf of the Maine Education Association, I want to thank you for taking time to participate in the Maine Education Association's Screening & Endorsement process. In Senate District 21, the MEA has endorsed the candidacy of Senator James Handy. The endorsement process in Senate District 21 was an extremely difficult decision for the local screening and endorsement interview team. Both Democratic incumbents have a solid record in support of public education.

> *The decision to endorse Senator Handy in the primary race was determined by his receipt of the Maine Teachers Association's Friend of Education Award in 1990, his past experience on the Education Committee, and his sponsorship of the Professional Standards Board for Teachers legislation in the 115th and 116th Legislatures.*
>
> *If you have any questions about the Screening & endorsement process, please contact Steven E. Crouse, Director of Government Relations and Political Action.*
>
> *Sincerely,*
Ann P. Anctil, President

The fair thing would have been for them to not endorse anyone in this case. The fact that Mr. Handy was my Senate seatmate did not make matters any easier although we continued to have a cordial and friendly relationship which superseded our divergent political views.

I then decided to send a letter to all the local teachers, which said:

> *Dear Educator:*
>
> *Since you influence the lives of tomorrow's leaders, your every professional need remains of utmost concern to me. Therefore, the reason for this letter.*
>
> *I realize that the Maine Education Association has chosen to endorse my opponent to represent District 21 in the Maine Senate even though our voting record is the same on education issues; however, our democratic system is wonderful...it allows us the freedom to choose. Hence, we all have this individual, very private privilege. I am reminded that the Association's decision does not necessarily reflect your choice.*
>
> *I very much want to continue representing you as together we work toward ensuring a happy today for you and bright future for our children.*
>
> *I would appreciate your vote on Tuesday, June 14th."*

The election results were heart-warming. We took every precinct including Mr. Handy's. While he worked hard in his campaign, which was managed by an experienced campaign worker who was also a state employee, the campaign was not nasty and he earned my respect. On my side were strictly volunteers who donated their time to walk with me throughout the District, standing at busy storefronts passing out my

Thank You, Georgette

literature. And now that the Primary was over I would prepare for another campaign against an aggressive Republican opponent.

A few days before the Primary, the Republican candidate (he was the only one in the Republican primary) Paul Madore came to my home. Paul Madore was conservative and, while we probably agreed on some issues, I did not support his approach, which was often vindictive and as others claimed, hateful. We sat at the dining room table that has also always served as my "office." One other person was present to hear this. Mr. Madore was concerned about the Primary and about Mr. Handy. He said: "Mrs. Bérubé, I know your positions on the issues and I feel the same way. I'm only in this election to oppose Jim Handy. If you win the Primary, I'm going to pull out."

I won the Primary. Again I was gratified by the support received by the voters. We had again captured all the precincts. The vote:

      BERUBE   3097
      HANDY   1770

For the next few months I continued to campaign for the General Election …as did Paul Madore …he would not prevail.

ABSENTEE BALLOTS

One means of getting a head start on the opponents was the blatant abuse of the absentee ballot process, especially in nursing homes and retirement facilities. A voter unable to go to the polling place on Election Day was and is allowed to vote by the absentee method. But first, that voter must sign an application form requesting a ballot. With that paper in hand, a campaign worker can receive the ballot from the City or Town Clerk's office and then proceed to have the voter cast a vote. Total privacy must be ensured to the voter.

More absentee ballots were cast in the City of Lewiston during the 1974 Primary election than in any other Maine community. Maine's largest city, Portland, cast 395 absentees or less than one percent of its total vote, while Lewiston counted 596 absentees. Maine at that time was also the only New England state to allow the handling of absentees by third parties. Most other states required that ballots be mailed directly to the prospective voter and mailed back to election officials. The following item in an October 1974 edition of the Lewiston Evening Journal was on mark:

> *Applications are of the 'fill in the back' variety and do not vary from year to year. As a result, some candidates process the applications months ahead of an election and some have been rumored to have been processed years ahead of an election. Some nursing homes and elderly housing residents cast 25% of their votes as absentee citing physical incapacitation as their reason for not being able to go to the polls; yet, that housing is not supposed to be for the physically incapacitated and in that case the voting place was only a short distance."*

In the 1980s and 1990s, legislation was passed to change the absentee method procedure to ensure fair play. These were victories against an entrenched political machine and which contributed to its demise.

In order to address the problem of "storage" of applications, I proposed to change the color of the application form for each election. That failed, and throughout the many attempts to address the abuses, opposition surfaced as expected from leaders of both parties as well as some municipal election officials. Finally, with the support of reform-minded legislators, a new law was enacted which said that henceforth the applications for an absentee ballot would be printed with the date of the election. Truly a victory for honest elections.

ISSUES AND PROGRAMS

NORTHERN IRELAND DIVESTITURE

One of the most interesting public hearings that I chaired during the 1990s dealt with the issue of discrimination in Northern Ireland. A bill was introduced which mandated that the Maine State Retirement System divest itself of stock it held in American companies doing business in Northern Ireland, unless those businesses subscribed to the MacBride Principles.

The nine MacBride Principles were aimed at containing the repression of Catholics in the workplace and thus open the doors of employment to more of that minority. One of these Principles stipulated that companies actively recruit Catholics; another would ban provocative religious or political emblems at the workplace. There was one which several members of the Committee, including myself, felt was most difficult to implement: to provide security from a worker's home in the Catholic district of West Belfast to the workplace and back. Many Catholics were reluctant to seek employment with American companies because they did not want to risk traveling through Protestant neighborhoods in order to reach the plants.

My concern was in the ability of American companies to implement the requirements of the Principles as well as to the cost to the State Retirement System in the process of divesting. Was there a better way to ensure that Catholics could access good paying jobs with American companies? While it was brought out that 4.2% of workers in these plants were indeed Catholics, none were in management positions. Ford Motor Company, for instance, already paid the highest wages and extended to its employees the same benefits as those given in the USA. It also actively recruited Catholics for all open positions, including management positions.

This legislation, introduced by Senator John Kerry of Saco, became a divisive and emotional issue, and to legislators of Irish descent, became a cause. The wood-paneled hearing room was filled to capacity. Proponents of the measure had strung up banners to support their position. Speakers for both sides had traveled from Northern Ireland to testify and also present, although only as observers, were staff from the British consulate in Boston.

The first speaker in favor of the bill, speaking after the presentation by the sponsor, was Father Sean McManus who was based in Washington, DC representing the interests of Sinn Fein, the political arm of the Irish Republican Army. His testimony was interspersed with vitriolic language. At one point, turning to the front row of spectators and looking straight at Paddy Devlin, a pro-labor member of the Northern Parliament and a Catholic who had come to speak against the legislation, with venom spewing from his mouth said: "You are an Uncle Tom." Devlin sat red-faced, visibly shocked and angry. The thought that popped into my head at that moment was: so much for Christian tolerance, especially from a Catholic priest.

Paddy Devlin has been described as a visionary, trade unionist, politician, man of the people. A rotund man, Mr. Devlin gained a reputation as a Catholic activist who sought freedom from Britain, but who also sought better working conditions for the people. He was a union organizer who had dedicated his life seeking a better one for his compatriots.

When it came time for the opponents to speak, Devlin slowly rose from his chair and walked to the podium. Silence fell like a death knell. He then proceeded with a recitation of the troubles in his homeland providing the Committee with historical data. He recounted marching in freedom parades and being jailed for his efforts and beliefs, all the while gaining an enviable reputation as defender of the working men and women. He remarked that good paying jobs were created by American companies. He proceeded to explain that newly-enacted laws, along with a new Human Rights Commission, were just beginning to be felt and that if American businesses were unable to operate under the restrictive MacBride Principles, the Catholic workers of Northern Ireland, the very people this legislation sought to support, would be the ones hurt.

He chastised the "Johnny Come Latelies" who lived in comfort outside of Ireland like Father McManus who is stationed in Washington DC. Then turning to the Reverend McManus, with disgust in his voice, said: "and you, sir, are a disgrace to the collar you wear." I fought hard not to applaud. His oratorical skills and convincing arguments split the Committee, which reported the bill as a divided report and it was on its way to the Senate.

The ensuing debate was civil but at times emotional. The sponsor, Senator John Kerry of Saco, argued eloquently for its passage. Still strong after his week long fast intended to bring attention to his proposal, he defended it and urged its passage. This all occurred on a very special day for the Irish Senators: March 17th, St. Patrick's Day. Leadership had accommodated Kerry's request that the debate take place on that date.

Both the Senate and the House accepted the Ought to Pass Committee report and it was sent to the Governor for his signature, but a subsequent veto by then-Governor McKernan was sustained by the Senate as it lacked the 2/3 vote of those present and voting which is needed and difficult to attain.

Civility reigned during the long debate. After the enacting vote, I rose and extended my congratulations to Senator Kerry. I reminded him, however, after listening to his remarks on the Saint whose feast day the Irish were celebrating, that he should be reminded that St. Patrick indeed was not an Irishman, but came from France and was sent to convert the 'heathens' of Hibernia...and I closed my remarks with: "ERIN GO BRAGH."

We shook hands.

SOUTH AFRICA BOYCOTT

One of the more interesting visitors to the State House during my tenure was the South African Ambassador to the United States, Harry Schwarz. He had come to meet privately with me as chair of the State and Local Government Committee. A public hearing was to be held on a proposal that would ban the purchase of goods from companies doing business in South Africa. The sponsors felt that sanctions would speed up the destruction of apartheid. Accompanied by the consular representative from Boston and a bodyguard, he wanted to share his concerns with the proposed legislation. This was a private visit on his part and was not publicized. Although I had asked the House co-chair to join us, she declined as she was a strong supporter of the bill.

Intelligent and well informed on our legislative process, the Ambassador argued his case for defeat of the legislation, citing his fears that the progress being made in ridding his country of apartheid would be placed in jeopardy if there were economic setbacks caused by these sanctions. If Maine enacted such a measure, it could have a domino effect with other States and thus bring economic chaos to that country. Rather than a peaceful transition, he mused, that change could come with bloodshed. The negative impact on his country would be devastating.

He recounted how he had been one of the lawyers defending Dr. Nelson Mandela at the time of the trial that condemned him to years in prison, and as though thinking aloud, the Ambassador said that: "I have never run away from a fight." He then corrected himself, "I take that back. At the age of 16 I ran away from Hitler and went to South Africa."

The bill came out of the Committee with a majority Ought to Pass report, but the Senate accepted the Ought Not to Pass minority report by a vote of 20-15. If enacted it would have prevented Maine from buying from local businesses handling goods of companies doing business in South Africa, companies such as Kellogg, Ford Motor Company, and IBM to name a few. For example, the State of Maine would be precluded from purchasing Ford products or replacement parts, yet could buy foreign products from such companies as Japanese-owned Toyota, who did business with South Africa. It did not make much sense to me that we would punish American businesses at retail or manufacturing. To avoid sanctions, American companies doing business in South Africa would conform and subscribe to the Sullivan Principles.

These were drafted by an American clergyman and dealt with the issue of discrimination and bias. While there were valid arguments in favor of a boycott, I nonetheless felt that economic retaliation against American-owned companies would hurt the very people the legislation sought to help: those living in poverty would bear the brunt of the sanctions and be deprived of good-paying jobs if the businesses were forced to leave.

Great strides were being made in 1991 by the DeKlerk government and sanctions as drastic as those proposed would hamper efforts toward a true democracy. As Ambassador Schwarz wrote in his book *Poverty Corrodes Freedom*, "Sanctions have had the effect of slowing down the single most important engine of change, South Africa's economy. Countries that embarked on a course of sanctions, disinvestments and other punitive measures to force change have a moral obligation to reverse that course now that their reasons for applying pressure have disappeared. Those who claim credit for the change also have to take responsibility for the damage they caused."

Though the Ought Not to Pass report had been accepted, it was later reversed with an Ought to Pass accepted. It died on the day of adjournment on July 10, 1991, but miraculously it was recalled from the legislative files and enacted. A subsequent veto by Governor John McKernan, however, was sustained.

LEWISTON-AUBURN THIRD BRIDGE

Like many other urban centers around the country, the Twin Cities of Lewiston-Auburn experienced increased traffic between the two communities which are separated by the beautiful Androscoggin River (beautified only after many years of abuse and pollution) and linked by two bridges. And so, consideration was given to floating a bond in order to build a third bridge. Funding was to be a minor problem compared to the real problem: what to name it! Was there any doubt as to whose name would be forever emblazoned in concrete?

Legislation was introduced to name it for "Mr. D," the long-serving legislator from Lewiston, Louis Jalbert. The sponsor was the Representative from Rumford, Mr. Fraser, and he did so at the request of Roger Mallar, Commissioner of the Department of Transportation, to lend his name and the strength of the Department to give it a measure of credibility.

The Transportation Committee endorsed the bill by a vote of 12-1, the lone dissenter being Republican Senator Greeley. There began torrents of praise, mostly from Republican members who felt beholden or were told they should be. They were lavish in their support of the Ought to Pass report. But during the debate in the House, looking around the chamber, one could see the looks of incredulity from members who sat listening to the floral language of praise of "Mr. D." One member intoned that he felt the name of Louis Jalbert Bridge was "not dignified enough" and suggested an amendment to name it the Louis Jalbert Memorial Bridge. He continued, "I suggested the name Memorial which is suitable for a person unless he was dead. Mr. Jalbert is far from dead: in fact, he is too much alive for some persons."

The Committee report was accepted without a vote and sent to the Senate a second time for their action. It was due for a rude awakening. Senator Joseph Brennan (later a two-term governor) said in debate that it was "terribly, terribly dangerous to name a bridge after living people." Senator Greeley was quoted as saying: "Louis Jalbert did a lot of work. He also is doing a lot of work to get it named after him."

Senator Carroll Minkowsky of Lewiston moved to indefinitely postpone the bill, effectively killing it. That in itself was an act of bravura. His motion was accepted without a recorded vote of 20-7 and it was sent to the House where the members insisted on their previous favorable action and the bill was returned to the Senate in non-concurrence. For

Thank You, Georgette

legislation to pass it must be approved by both chambers and signed by the Governor.

A competing measure was presented to name this new bridge the Vietnam Veterans' Memorial Bridge. The same Committee voted 12-1 against this new proposal, with once again Senator Greely being the lone Committee member to vote in support. The bill was again brought to the House. The Republican representative from Bath, Rodney Ross, said: "There is no individual that did as much work for the third bridge in Lewiston as Representative Jalbert. To assure the approval of the voters in referendum, he made at least two complete tours of the state. He wore himself out and he ended up for two weeks in what he calls his third home, Lewiston's St. Mary's General Hospital," he thundered. It became apparent that support for the Vietnam name was eroding. References to the tours had many disbelievers.

Much of the opposition to the new name came from Jalbert supporters. On the other hand, those who favored the Vietnam name were described as leading a "vendetta against Jalbert." Much was not said publicly.

A Senator came to see me in the House and asked that I try to have the measure tabled in order to give the Senate time to kill the original bill, the name of Jalbert Bridge. "Georgette," he said, "we just cannot have this bridge named for a convicted felon."

I agreed to do so realizing that I was going to attract retaliation from some quarters – and from Louis Jalbert who was a member of the powerful Appropriations Committee. But, nonetheless, at the right moment I stood and moved a tabling motion, and to my surprise it was accepted.

That night, or rather early in the morning at approximately 12:45 a.m., the phone at my house rang and a male voice said: "You are trying to kill the bridge…you'd better vote right tomorrow." It was with apprehension that I arrived at the State House ready to debate the issue. That afternoon Mr. Jalbert stood on the floor and asked that the Jalbert bill not pass. He said that he had not asked for the bridge to be named for him, that now he was going home. He then proceeded to slowly walk out of the House, but once outside the glass doors instead of walking in the corridor, he slipped into the Speaker's office adjacent to the House where he listened over the loudspeaker to the debate and its final outcome.

The bill died, and immediately the legislation calling for a Vietnam Veterans' Memorial Bridge was brought forward, passed, and after concurrence with the Senate, became law. Those of us who had supported honoring our military veterans survived and gradually watched the erosion of power of a political machine no longer. And in all those years, that paper tiger had succeeded only in instilling fear. During the debate I said

Georgette B. Bérubé

that naming the bridge for our veterans "would be a constant reminder that this sad episode in our history – the Vietnam War – will never be repeated, and that it will always be reminder of the tragedy of war."

It was not the war that my husband had fought in, in which our country was attacked and we responded to secure our democracy – but the soldiers who fought in Vietnam answered their country's call as well and so deserved respect and remembrance.

TOBACCO 'STING' PROGRAM

Tobacco, like other addictive substances, must be taken out of the hands of children and young adults. To help achieve this goal, there is a federally funded program whereby young people aged 15 to 17 years of age are hired and used in 'sting' operations. They are brought to stores where they attempt to purchase cigarettes. If they succeed, the owner is fined. LD2052 was legislation that would have prohibited the practice of using teenagers.

In these operations, the youth is brought to a store by a law-enforcement officer, he/she carries no identification, and has just enough money to make one purchase. The juvenile, once he/she is sold the pack, immediately leaves and turns over the cigarettes to the officer who then enters the premises and charges the owner. The fine starts at $250. No cameras record the transaction; there are no eyewitnesses. If the clerk refuses to sell a pack, the teen-ager leaves immediately without a word. For this, the young people are paid $7.25 per hour.

The only opponents to this bill, that is those who wanted to retain the practice, were an employee of the Department of Mental Health, Mental Retardation and Substance Abuse, and a State House lobbyist who said that he was speaking as a private citizen. What he neglected to say was that he was an officer of No Nicotine Inc., which held a contract with the Department of Human Services to manage this program.

At the public hearing, the Committee was told that parents are delighted to sign over their permission for their 15-year old to be part of this entrapment program. What we do not hear is that they also sign a release for liability in case their child is hurt. The contracting agent has no risk. Also, the parent must assume the cost of medical expenses in the event their child is injured.

Of the 500 establishments visited, only 11 allegedly sold the kids cigarettes, according to testimony.

I supported the bill to prohibit youngsters from participating in this program. I thought that entrapment was wrong and sets a bad example. But worse in my mind was using juveniles in this work. We all agree that smoking is harmful; but if indeed it is, why not simply stop all sales of tobacco? The cynical answer would be that there would be a loss of millions in tobacco tax revenue, as well as Federal funds coming into our state. If tobacco is an addictive substance, then the lure of governmental funding is also a very powerful habit-forming matter.

The bill failed.

FAROG

When money flows freely into the coffers of the state, proposals are received from many varied sources as to how those dollars can be put to good use…often the 'good use' is merely a job-creating means for those who come up with new ideas…some good, some not so good.

One such proposal, well-intentioned, was advanced by a young man in 1971 who thought that it would be beneficial to the Franco-American students at the Orono campus of the University of Maine if there were a center to help them acclimate to their new college environment. Yvon Labbé felt that young people of French-Canadian or Acadian backgrounds had always been discriminated against and that it was imperative that an office be created to assist them in the transition from home to the foreign land of higher education. In exploring this further, I could not find a single student of Canadian heritage who could not speak English; yet with the politically-appealing word 'Franco,' he succeeded in receiving funding from the University for a center to be called the Franco-American Resource Opportunity Group (FAROG) and three decades later he is still its one and only paid director.

While FAROG had a few strong supporters, it also was criticized for being outside the mainstream particularly in its promotion of the varieties of local French language. Its main direction was to further the dialects of French spoken in various regions of Maine, while its detractors felt that teaching of an international French might serve the users better, especially since most did not speak the *patois* language of their parents and grandparents.

In 1989, bill LD1552 was proposed to establish yet another francophone center within the University with the purpose of advancing the language, culture and heritage of the French in Maine. As director Yvon Labbé stated in a Bangor Daily News article, "we have to give back to the French what has been taken away, and one of the prime examples is that French is taught as a foreign language, and that means that your language is no longer 'your language'."

In all my years of living in Maine, and being a member of this French population, I was amazed at never having known what it was that had been taken away from me, nor that the French language was no longer mine. I don't ever recall having been the victim of prejudice or someone laughing at me for not being able to speak English as I entered school.

Funding for this piece of legislation was pegged at $400,000 for the first year to create the center, plus $100,000 for an archival preservation center at the University campus in Fort Kent. But with little support from the Legislature, the bill was withdrawn.

Prior to its withdrawal, a letter was received by members of the Senate from FAROG which included one telling sentence: 'it is crucial to all of us that the Franco-American population be served and not merely used." FAROG had become a vocal activist group advocating ways to eliminate problems where none existed.

However, what took the eyes of Senators in that letter was the imprint of the University phone number for the FAROG office: (207) 581-FROG…and on taxpayer-paid stationery and postage. Several Senators who had constituents of French-Canadian descent were offended by a word that was as demeaning as other pejorative words describing other ethnicities and races.

A letter was sent to the signers of the FAROG letter, Ms. Stiles and director Labbé, indicating any inappropriateness of this word. A call made to the Chancellor's office resulted in the elimination of the offensive word. The Senators' letter read:

> *We the undersigned elected officials representing large populations of citizens of French ancestry take umbrage with your letter of May 23,1989 mailed under the auspices of the Centre Franco-Américain at the University of Maine. Particularly offensive to us is the pejorative word "FROG' which you incorporated in your telephone number, rather than the much more common numbers. This telephone acronym is most inappropriately associated with the Centre Franco-Américain within the University system. The use of the word FROG does a grave disservice to the many proud and industrious French-speaking citizens of Maine; furthermore, its use undermines the significant contributions and tremendous progress that has been achieved by this segment of Maine's population over these many years.*
>
> *In employing this acronym, those at the Centre Franco-Américain may have thought that the best way to neutralize a distasteful epithet was with sardonic, self-deprecating wit. Conversely, it is our contention that it serves only to make them appear clownish by trying to light-heartedly wear the demeaning caricature created by others. Whatever the motive, the term is still repugnant, even emotionally upsetting to many of us who endured its barbs and experienced unwarranted pain as it was historically used in a blatantly uncomplimentary and/or insulting manner to describe Franco-Americans.*

Georgette B. Bérubé

> *The continued use of this word in your letterhead does not strike us as a constructive way to bring the Franco-American community together or, even more importantly, to promote pride in our culture and heritage.*
>
> *The courtesy of your prompt attention to this matter, as well as your response to this letter, will be greatly appreciated."*

This illustrates how programs start, and once funded, become very difficult to monitor in order to know how the taxpayers' monies have been spent and whether those dollars have accomplished their goal. Too often, however, funding comes not because it is justifiable but because there are catchy words like *child, elderly, Franco, clean (elections) environment,* etc., or even better: *federal/state dollars are available.*

A response to the letter was received from a Gérard Normand Paré, as well as from Yvon Labbé and Deborah Stiles employed at that office. The letter from Paré read:

> *I am sending this letter in response to your letter written to Yvon Labbé and Deborah Stiles at the Franco-American center. Your letter's focus was on symbols; you put down our symbol of the frog of which we are very proud. Now it is time for my stabs at your symbol (appearing on your letterhead). The State of Maine seal is very insulting to me because it reminds me of the WASP repression I saw as a child. The State of Maine seal very nicely depicts every aspect of Maine but one. The seal does not show anything about the French heritage which is prevalent in this state. Why is there not a fleur-de-lis anywhere on the State Seal? Another thing: why not write Je Dirige?*
>
> *Few people actually realize Maine is of French origin, there is a province in France named MAINE.*
>
> *Our symbol of the frog is our way of accepting our French roots and our ancestry. We should always remember where we came from. I was born in Vassalboro, Maine, a very WASP community. I was brought up bilingually and biculturally, which made it difficult when I went to school; everyone picked on me for my French name, and my English teachers tried changing Gérard Normand Paré to Gerald Norman Perry. The first is my name, thank you. The latter belongs to an imposter. The negative energy I got from them I used for pride in myself.*
>
> *My roots are very French. They go back to the 1500's to a French surgeon Ambroise Pare. My mother's family history goes*

back as far. My grandparents worked in the mill or garages or whatever they could find. Most importantly they worked very hard. I know that many Franco-Americans come from families who have seen hardship. They should be proud because it is families like theirs who show what the spirit of America is all about. They fought the wars, they worked the industries, and they provided food through farming; most of all they left part of their culture, which is very rich in tradition..

Any Franco-American, whether in the public eye or not, who cannot be proud of this very rugged, hard-working and unique French culture should not call themselves Franco-Americans, because they are denigrating their own heritage. If we say that we are of this culture we should not be ashamed of the frog, which itself is an amphibian, able to live both on land and water (bicultural). If we remember where we have come from we can use that energy to move ahead.

Vive la culture des Franco-Américains.

A contagious disease is pervading our state. Anything 'ethnic' is 'in' and often because Federal and State grants are available. Admittedly this is strong motivation to start up a new program aimed at 'Francos'. It is amazing how often Franco-Americans are sought after since they are the largest ethnic group in Maine. However, they are first Americans, as are those who come from Europe, Asia, Middle East, Far East, or Africa. Most do not wallow in issues of discrimination because they are too busy getting a start in a new life away from political instability or economic deprivation. That is not to say that immigrants have forsaken their culture but they know that in America, to succeed, they must adapt to the ways of their new country. One's culture and language should not supersede Americanism nor, by the same token, be tossed aside. Instead, they should be nurtured within their population for they know better how to retain and perpetuate their language, music, art, and all that enhances their traditions.

Cultural heritage should not be buried but kept alive as we all learn from one another's cultural backgrounds. I cannot speak to discrimination as I have never been a victim growing up, in school, or in my public life. A few years ago when I was asked by a young lady doing work on a grant on 'Francos' how often I had been the butt of jokes or discriminated against, I replied that I had never been subjected to this great wrong that is leveled at people. She hardly believed me, and maintained that she had been and still was a victim of such slurs. The interview ended abruptly: nothing to write about. One should wonder how a Request for Proposal had been written to allow for tax money to be handed out on this subject once again.

PETITIONS

The right to petition our government is inherent to democracy. To make it difficult if not unattainable to get the required signatures was often employed by that same government of the people, since this might be a challenge to the authority of and thus seen as placing more power in the hands of the electorate. The right to petition includes the circulation of petitions often used to lead into a citizens' initiated referendum.

In Lewiston, if a petition were initiated for a local issue it could not be circulated city-wide. It could only be signed in the office of the City Clerk thus making it virtually impossible to acquire the needed signatures necessary to place a question on the ballot. Those wishing to sign had to go to City Hall, climb to the second floor and affix their signature for all to see, including the press. Signers' names were then printed in the daily evening newspaper. As a result of these deterrents it is easy to see why it was unlikely that such a petition could actually be successful. But if citizens were motivated enough by the issue involved, these obstacles could be overcome.

One such petition called for a referendum to allow the voters of Lewiston to vote on whether they favored the closing of a section of Campus Avenue in order to allow St. Mary's General Hospital to build a walkway across the street to their nursing home. Surprisingly hundreds of citizens trouped to the Clerk's office to sign. The necessary signatures were gathered, a referendum was held, the street-closing proposal defeated.

This process of denying the privilege to circulate any petition city-wide seemed undemocratic to me and so I drafted legislation which would allow residents of a municipality to circulate a petition for a local issue outside of the City Building. The proposal went to the State and Local Government Committee. Unbelievably, the only opponents were Lewiston's City Clerk and the City Manager of Portland, both representing the only two communities in the state to ban the circulation of petitions for municipal issues.

The Committee accepted this legislation unanimously. But the opponents approached me asking that I withdraw the bill with the promise that they might be able to work on a compromise. I declined and my bill became law.

STUDIES

Here are two examples of requests for funds to conduct "studies." They illustrate how so often monies are spent with very little apparent benefit to the citizens of this state. Perhaps, though, the beneficiaries are advocates of a cause, who can then point to a study as indicative of a great need for some change, or better still, funding to cure whatever may ail the cause.

The title of one study: "Resolve, Creating a Commission to Study the Multicultural Education Needs of Maine Teachers to Ensure Cultural Awareness and Understanding for all Maine Students"! Members of the study commission would represent the following groups: Passamaquoddy Tribe, Penobscot Indian Nation, African-Americans and Franco-Americans. The cost? $17,000 subsequently revised downward to $14,000. While such a study might have proven useful at the time of the great migration from French Canada and other countries as well as at the turn of the 20th century and through its early decades, it might be difficult to justify today on the basis of need, since in the case of Franco-Americans, now in their 2nd, 3rd, and 4th generations, these descendants carry French surnames yet most do not speak the language of their forefathers.

With only one person from the Department of Education speaking in favor of passage, other than the sponsors, none spoke in opposition. How could they? Mercifully this proposal was killed for lack of funding, but was re-introduced in a future session.

The second example is more telling. Often we find that some beneficiaries, also known as "special interest groups," spend an enormous amount of time dreaming up new programs. Always, of course, they are to be participants in whatever endeavor is planned. It assures them that their ideas will be included in a report. With a favorable report in hand their task is made easier in appealing for funds always necessary to carry this out.

This study title was "An Act to Foster Economic Growth Through the Recognition and Development of Maine's Franco-American Resource." It carried a fiscal note of $50,500 to be spent in the following manner: personnel ($1,100) all other ($1,500) Franco-American Center at Orono, to support its participation and expenses of members ($47,400), base allocation ($500)

Strategies:
1) Include French language and cultural heritage of Maine as an integral part of the way we define Maine's economic competitive advantage to the outside world.

2) Give a high priority to the preservation of Maine's traditional bilingual capability by the education system.
3) Monitor the condition of Maine's (French) resource – its language and people – on a regular basis.
4) Establish a data base

Actions:
1) Governor should establish by Executive Order a one-year interagency task force to begin the implementation of the above strategies.
2) Legislature should allocate the balance of funds not expended by this Commission to the Franco-American Center at Orono.

Although it was required in the proposed legislation to have the Legislature decide where the unexpended funds should go (perhaps back to the State Treasury would have been simple) no such directive was given and the Commission turned over the unspent $23,000 to the Franco Center at Orono. Can anyone honestly and unequivocally state that this study served the citizens of this state? It is one thing to fund wishes for programs; however, it is not so easy to know how monies are spent by private non-profit groups, and we might also include the private sector. It is imperative that all recipients conform to accountability rules. In this case, the spending figures were hard to come by, and only after going to the higher authorities at the university were we able to get them. This is how the $50,500 was spent:

Activity	FY'97-98	FY'98-99
U/M Faculty Research projects		3,390.88
Visiting artist, and FAROG theater project		4,387.06
U/Laval, U/M, CD ROM Commerce Research		8,759.00
Communications	1,950.00	2,438.79
Maine/Beauce Initiatives		764.76
Forum Francophone des Affaires	6,703.07	
(support for Vietnam & Washington trips)	2,265.36	
Travel International and Domestic	4,615.85	
	8,304.17	2,022.72
	2,184.54	1,533.45
	26,022.99	23,296.66

Accountability would have shown that the expenditures did not conform to the original intent of the proposal. Not all studies are irrelevant. Many have served good purposes in addressing key issues and as a result some statutes have been made more effective particularly in areas of

Georgette B. Bérubé

environment, social services and child welfare. In this case, some expenses were made after the report had been printed. This is totally unacceptable.

The following is a partial list of those who traveled out of the country and state on this grant; some were not members of the study commission:

According to the study report, five meetings were held through a six-month period during which the $50,500 was spent. The end result? A ten-page report made up of the following:

1 page	The Global Francophone Opportunity
1 ½ pages	Current State Initiatives (festivals, etc)
1 ½ pages	Maine's French-speaking population
2 pages	Three long-term strategies
1 page	French ancestry by County
1 page	Selective Publications
1 page	Acknowledgments
1 page	by Place

All information gathered on these 10 pages could have been obtained from the Law Library at the State House at no cost. Although it was clearly stated in the legislation passed for this study that the Legislature would be the one to determine where the unexpended funding should go, instead the Commission turned over the unspent $23,000 to the Franco Center at the University of Maine at Orono. No accounting was ever made as to how the surplus was spent. It appears that none of the strategies and recommendations was implemented except the one to turn over the unexpended study funds to the Franco Center at University of Maine in Orono. No doubt this would have been too costly.

Thank You, Georgette

NAME	DATE	COST	DESTINATION	PURPOSE OF TRIP
Tony Brinkley	8/4/97	37.12	Boston	Forum Francophone
	9/23/97	678.00	Washington, D.C.	Congressional Delegation Meeting
	10/4/97	2993.00	Hanoi	Trade Delegation Meeting
	10/17/97	649.07	Boston	Vietnam Project
Yvon Labbé	7/20/97	263.20	Québec	Ministry International Relations
	9/14/97	30.29	St.Georges, Canada	Commerce Initiative Meeting
	9/30/97	175.51	St.Georges, Canada	U/M Partnership Mtg.
Lisa Michaud	10/22/97	354.24	St.Georges, Canada	Studies French Immersion
Long Ngo	10/5/97	2,194.00	Ho Chi Minh City	Trade Delegation Meeting
Lisa Michaud	3/14/98	139,55	St.Georges	Int'l Exch. Comm
	3/15/98	203.63	Québec	Tourism Comm Meeting
	4/27/98	656.95	Québec	French speaking Skills Conference
	7/19/98	150.00	Québec	Recruiting faculty
	8/10/98	215.16	Québec	Bilateral Meeting
	3/26/98	300.00	Québec	Foster Grandparents Program
Joseph Cyr	9/12/98	263.25	Caraquet, NB	Culture Project
Dean Louder	9/26/98	140.02	Québec	Franco-American Staff Meeting
	12/18/98	125.00	Québec	Franco-American Staff Meeting
	1/8/99	87.70	Québec	Academic Council. Meeting
Yvon Labbé	8/18/98	500.00	Montreal	Int'l Assoc.Parliamentarians *
	11/13/98	164.51	Québec	Language Immersion
Michael Grillo	7/6/98	580.00	New Brunswick, NJ	Faculty Immersion Program

*It should be noted that this association is only open to French-speaking elected officials (parliamentarians) who attend conferences held in French-speaking countries. The Maine Legislature has been a member.

61

PARTISANSHIP / PERSONALITIES

"John L. Martin. One of the most interesting figures in Maine political history…sometime adversary but always a personal friend."

JOHN L. MARTIN

John L. Martin: inflated ego, pompous, domineering, controlling, rude, childish, insecure…all accurate adjectives, all reported in the press. But in these thirty years I also knew John to be compassionate, sensitive, a brilliant politician and orator, a parliamentarian extraordinaire, with a deep love – though sometimes misplaced – for the democratic process.

A master at conducting legislative sessions, John always insisted that decorum be maintained, that the dress code be enforced, and that no off-color language permitted during debate. Members were not allowed to bring food into the House chamber, and if he spotted someone munching, he would dispatch a page to ask them to stop or leave. He was a stickler for protocol. From the vantage point of the podium he could assess the mood of his chamber; he could also sense the "games" that were sometimes being played. For example, one forenoon he noticed that notes were being passed, and as these notes were received, heads would turn toward a woman member, and knowing smiles would appear. He soon figured out what was going on. He summoned a page and told him to ask the Representative to go change her "too *décolleté*" blouse or to find a jacket to cover her "buxomy" chest. The notes ceased and so did the smiles.

No one ever succeeded in winning on a challenge to John's rulings on points of order. "The Chair rules" was his stark and imperious reply to anyone pointing to Mason's Rules of Order to bolster their argument. On one occasion, a Republican legislator rose to ask a clarification of a ruling by the presiding officer, and he added that he thought John had erred. The Speaker reiterated his opinion and stated that he stood by it. "But," said the hapless Representative holding up a copy of Mason's, "may I quote from the book," obviously pushing his luck as the Speaker simmered at the podium, glaring from his lofty perch, "Mason's says that your ruling is incorrect," and before he could continue, the gavel came thundering down on the mahogany rostrum. (John had a storied history of breaking gavels.) "The Representative will kindly sit down or I will instruct the Sergeant-at-Arms to escort him from the Chamber." End of discussion.

The quest for power can also be attributed to one's own insecurity. This often translates into using fear for persuasion rather than using the strength of an issue. This is illustrated by a call I received from Speaker Martin.

A bill that he supported had been given an Ought Not to Pass report by the State and Local Government Committee which I chaired. This report was on the Senate calendar for that day. John asked that I recommit it to Committee so that he could have another shot at getting an Ought to Pass

Georgette B. Bérubé

report instead. The extra time would allow him to speak to the opposing members hoping to change their position. I responded that we had held a four-hour public hearing on this bill and that there was not much support in Committee, even after we held an unusual three work sessions. And that if we re-referred it, that the outcome would be the same. He insisted and added, "if the Democrats don't change their minds, I'll remove them from that Committee."

I said that I agreed with the opposition view. Before I could continue, he cut in with "you're nothing but a g.d. (expletive deleted) Republican." The loud slam at the other end told me that the conversation had ended. I did not move to recommit the legislation and it died a painless death. Threats were never carried out. Later that day as I was walking in the corridor, he passed me, stopped and placed his arm around my shoulder. All was well again.

Many things have been written about Representative Martin especially during his final tenure as Speaker when a question about ballot tampering was raised. Depicted as a power-hungry tyrant, he was seldom described by his many acts of kindness. He would take great effort in helping a staff member who might have personal problems or a student with not enough money to continue his or her education. I recall one female Republican Representative who lacked three months of service to qualify for a state retirement pension when she left office. John, hearing this, found her a temporary job in his office and later said that she had been one of the best staff persons he had ever had. He was always available to any member of his caucus as well as to members of the opposition. Helping even a member of the opposition was never publicized. To paraphrase Congressman Thomas "Tip" O'Neil, Speaker of the U.S. House of Representatives, in remarks about former President Ronald Reagan: "He would have made a hell of a king." John knew the legislative process inside and out, and he insisted on knowing every small incident or problem that plagued the members. He took an interest in every issue.

Few ever took issue with Speaker Martin and came out victorious. After all, who would want to jeopardize a pet legislation project or lose out on a trip to some far away state or country?

One of my favorite legislators and a friend as well was the grand lady from Brunswick, Representative Antoinette "Tony" Martin. She debated from the heart, never speaking from notes, and speaking in language that everyone understood. She was one of the most effective members, I must add.

On one occasion, in the heat of a debate on a bill that would have allowed the hunting of bear with traps - a method to which she was

Thank You, Georgette

adamantly opposed - she used the word "damn." Before she could utter another word, the Speaker's gavel came thundering down and she was admonished from the podium. It should be noted here that John assumed the Speakership at a very young age – by the time I arrived in January 1971 he had already served two terms and was still in his mid-twenties.

Not to be outdone, from the height of her imposing stature, Tony quickly said in an equally thunderous voice: "Mr. Speaker, you're not going to tell me what and what not to say, nor intimidate me. I learned to swear in the textile mills when you were still in diapers." Laughter and applause greeted her remark. John calmed down, smiled, and then burst out laughing. He had met his match.

As often happens to persons in authority, would-be court jesters were always present at his elbow saying how great he was. In my view this was doing him a great disservice. Their words of adulation should have been to offer constructive criticism when appropriate to do so.

On one occasion the Democrat members of the State and Local Government Committee were summoned to his office for instructions on how to proceed on a particular bill before the Committee. In his jovial manner he cracked a joke and the "wannabes" laughed, some out-laughing their colleagues. I did not laugh and continued to take notes. John noticed, then said in his Acadian French dialect:

"*Tu ris pas?*" (You're not laughing?)

"No, John, it wasn't that funny."

"*C'est bon, c'est bon*" he replied (it's good, it's good).

He then hugged me and we returned to the issue at hand.

John was quick with a reply and he always had the last word. Once as I stood up to speak on a bill that he opposed, there suddenly was interference in the sound system. Music and a voice came over the loudspeakers. I interrupted myself to question if this could be fixed so that I could continue my remarks without being distracted by a freak radio signal. Quick as a flash the Speaker, looking up to the sky, said it was a hint from the Almighty to stop my speech. I could not let him get away with this, especially with the laughter it provoked.

"But, Mr. Speaker, I thought you were Him." More laughter. John smiled.

Many stories have been written about the "Count of Aroostook County," but none as biting or as rancorous as in his last days as Speaker of the House. His supporters had turned against him. It became easier to stomp on the fallen leader once he was down. The about face of his former allies and supporters plus the negative press could not help but hurt him personally. However, he never displayed any anger nor did he seek retaliation. To some members, the fear of losing their coming elections because of their association with John L. Martin was too much of a risk. To some winning an election superseded loyalty.

The King is dead…long live the King. This was never more noticeable than during the last months that he spent as an ordinary Representative after he relinquished his post and all the trappings that come with the office. No more ever-present entourage, no more private office or staff to do his bidding. He was alone. But lost also was his tremendous knowledge and it was not unusual to see his colleagues asking him for advice which he willingly gave.

As the British Prime Minister Benjamin D'Israeli wrote: "…all power is a trust; that we are accountable for its exercise; that from the people, and for the people all springs, and all must exist."

Too soon do we forget history instead of learning from it.

But John is a survivor. At the time of this writing, he has risen to serve in the Maine State Senate. And I would not be surprised to eventually see him selected as President of that body.

104TH BIRTHDAY

To illustrate to what degree partisanship exists in some quarters: a State Representative from Auburn called the office of the Senate Majority Leader, Senator Nancy Clark of Freeport and a Democrat, to report that I had my picture in the morning newspaper with Representative Albert Stevens, a Republican from Sabattus, one of the towns next to Lewiston. The caller expounded on the fact that I was consorting with members of the opposition Party. I was infuriated, particularly since the call came from one of the most ineffective members of the Legislature by all accounts.

I went to the office of my leader, Senator Clark whose fairness, intelligence and knowledge of issues I greatly respected. After relating my story she said that she was already aware of the call but was not pursuing the issue. Smiling, she added: "This could only come from Lewiston or Auburn."

The incriminating evidence? A photograph taken with a Republican colleague and two of our constituents from the town of Sabattus. I had been invited to attend a 104th birthday party for a lady who had achieved longevity. Since Sabattus at the time was in my Senate district, it was right that I should be present. I had thoroughly enjoyed visiting with her and sharing the ice cream and soda with her and her family. But to some, this was a no-no. Before I left, Senator Clark said: "Georgette, you did the right thing and I would have done the same."

DEMOCRAT YES, REPUBLICAN NO

Legislators are always eager to have constituents visit the State House. Many come, especially school children. When they do, they are given mementos of their visit such as lobster, apple or potato pins, and informative registers which include pictures of legislators as well as information on the legislative process.

On this particular occasion, my Republican seatmate, Senator Raynold Theriault from Fort Kent in Aroostook County, was hosting a large group of students from his district, quite a trip for a one-day visit to the Capitol. Senator Theriault asked me if I could spare a few registers to give to his young visitors as he only had a very few left. He also said that he had been unable to get more from the legislative post office. I gave him the few that I had and went to get more, and was told that they would be placed on my desk shortly. I must add that at that time the Democrats were the majority Party in the Senate. I was asked if I wanted my name stamped on each one. I declined saying they were for my seatmate…my big mistake.

It wasn't long before the Democratic Representative from that district came charging into the Senate chamber inquiring why I was giving these registers to a Republican. She had apparently not been told that there were visitors from the County. My answer simply was that even though we "D's" controlled the Senate, these booklets were printed to be given out and were paid for by all of our Maine taxpayers.

The registers were indeed given out, but under the stamped name of the irate Representative.

WORST EXPERIENCE

One of the worst experiences occurred when I became House Chair of the Audit and Program Review Committee in 1975. It was also my task to hire the Committee clerk. After reviewing and interviewing applicants, I selected a lady who had legislative experience and came highly recommended from both Parties. She worked out extremely well.

A few weeks into the session I was called into the office of the Clerk of the House, Edwin Pert, who also was in charge of the House staff and clerks among his many duties. He ran a tight ship with great efficiency and was to remain as a most effective Clerk for several years. Along with the election of the Constitutional officers, the Clerk is also elected by the House legislators, and in this case, the Democrat majority controlled this post as well. He proceeded to tell me that the clerk whom I had hired was a Republican.

"So?" I said.

He continued by saying that I should have hired a Democrat. Little had I thought that I had to ask a person's political affiliation. I relied on experience, ability and know-how. I responded by telling him that of the nine persons who had applied, two could not type, five had no idea of the legislative process, and one told me that she could not work after 3 p.m., which was a problem. We needed an assistant who could remain throughout public hearings that often extended to 5 p.m. and beyond.

Nonetheless, I was instructed to let her go. I was told that as an experienced clerk she had to be aware of the unwritten rules. For the next two days I could not bring myself to tell her. In later years, I would simply have told the Clerk that no way would I do this. But, being new to the process, I followed marching orders.

She graciously accepted the loss of her job but the tears in her eyes told me that this was disastrous to her. I promised myself that never again would I crumble to partisan "unwritten" rules. There has never been a truer saying than: "To the victor belongs the spoils."

LEGISLATION

GAMES OF CHANCE

A bill was introduced (LD833) in 1997 that would have banned slot machines. After holding a public hearing the Legal Affairs Committee gave it an Ought Not to Pass report by a slim divided vote, it then went to the House for its views and decision. The opponents of the proposal did not want to eliminate slots primarily because the state did derive some revenue from such sources as fees, and several charitable non-profit organizations stood to lose the income which they used for helping children and other worthy causes. Testimony in both the House and the Senate mentioned Maine State Police statistics on revenue brought in by these machines as $4.2 million by the year 1997. The opposition came mainly from social groups, veterans' organizations and lobbyists for the distributors.

On May 14 1979, the Ought to Pass minority report of the Committee was accepted by a narrow margin of 56 to 67. But the very next day, when it had been "softened," the vote was 70 to 66, this time to accept the Ought Not to Pass motion. Overnight, the vote had been reversed. It then proceeded to the Senate where the amended House version was accepted by a vote of 26 to 5. Since the two chambers disagreed, the bill would die if the House opposed the Senate. The final version was accepted by the Senate and sent back t the House. This time, on the motion to enact, the vote was 88 to 52. It was signed by the Senate President and was sent to the Governor for his signature.

All legislation passed that will cause a loss of revenue or will necessitate funding in order to be implemented must sit on what is referred to as the Appropriations Table. On the last two days of the session the Appropriations Committee and the Legislative Council vote to either allow or disallow the fiscal note. If the bill passed by the Legislature is not funded, then it does not become law. The Council is composed of the presiding officers of the House and Senate (Speaker and President), as well as the eight members who serve in leadership positions in both parties. It is at this point that many 'chits' are called. Therefore, this newly enacted law was to sit on the table with all the new laws calling for fiscal notes.

In this particular instance, I had heard that this legislation would not appear on the Appropriations Table but would be taken off prior to the end of the session and that money would be found immediately to fund the loss of revenue. And it happened. To my mind this action would be totally wrong and so on the day after the enactment on May 24, 1979 I addressed this issue on the floor of the House:

"For the past couple of days, I have been following very closely the Senate calendar's back page under 'Special Appropriations Table'. Yesterday bill LD833 was on the list with sixty other LD's waiting to be funded with surplus monies for a total of $13.2 million. This morning, it was the first item I looked for, and lo and behold, it had vanished. I was told that it had been taken off the table. I was further given a copy of the Portland Press Herald and I will quote from the last paragraph: 'we slipped it off the Appropriations Table and enacted it under the hammer in less than 20 seconds, said the Senate Majority leader.' (under the hammer means that it passed without a vote but being enacted when the presiding officer, the President, bangs the gavel.)

I do understand that leadership was divided, that it was not a unanimous decision. This bill had a fiscal cost because of a loss of revenue. Now I supported LD833 because I felt then, as I do now, that it was the right thing to do, but when I raised the issue some 10 days ago of the propriety of taking a bill out of order before the process was completed, I was told "that won't happen" and not to worry. I do take issue with the manner in which priority was determined. I think that slot machines were wrong, but two wrongs have never made a right nor have the ends justified the means. You know, to many the word 'politician' is equated with all that is wrong in our system. It doesn't have to be so. But as long as we must pass legislation at all costs, I feel that tactics such as this will create more disillusionment from the general public and lessen the conscientiousness of others who are involved, like us, in this process called government."

The House chairman of the Appropriations Committee rose and said: "Mr. Speaker: Ladies and Gentlemen of the House. I regret to hear the words from Mrs. Bérubé. I expected that it would be on the table like everything else, and I did not know that it was off the table." The Majority leader, James Tierney, also spoke:

"I think the gentlelady from Lewiston, Mrs. Bérubé, is absolutely correct in her characterization of the situation. I personally think it was unfortunate and I hope it won't happen again, but I think the members of the House certainly deserve an explanation.

The issue came up in leadership meetings and it was a divided leadership. I think I was the only one, maybe there were two of us, who felt that the bill should not be taken off the table and I lost, but that is not the point. The point is that the House should have known prior to enactment of that bill that it was not going to be tabled. That was wrong. I certainly give you my personal pledge, for what that is worth, that that situation will not be repeated."

The moral of the story: elected officials must resist playing to leaders and must be held accountable by the electorate. When an unethical act is allowed to occur, if there is prior knowledge, the silence of some taints everyone.

FORUM FRANCOPHONE DES AFFAIRES

LD1636, an ACT to RENEW MAINE'S ECONOMY was introduced with an initial request for $240,000 to establish an office of the Forum Francophone des Affaires in Lewiston. This would presumably enable this new agency to establish economic exchanges with French-speaking nations around the globe. The funding request was cut to $100,000 for the year 1997 and included in the Part II budget, commonly known as the supplemental budget. It included de-appropriations and new funding. The office would be set up in Lewiston. According to the language in the budget, this was to be "one-time" funding from the Maine taxpayers. This startup money would suffice while funding was sought from the business community.

It is interesting to note that in the following fiscal year, after heavy lobbying, the words "one-time" were replaced with "on-going," meaning that funding must be appropriated automatically in a budget. Here again there was no detailed accounting of how the state dollars had been spent in that first year. With the office closed off and on, and only one staff person, nothing concrete had been accomplished unless trips to Vietnam, Washington, and Europe were counted as positive activities.

The Governor's veto was not overridden in the Senate, failing to get the needed 2/3 votes to pass. The funding was changed to allow the Forum $75,000 and the same amount to the Maine International Trade office which would seek a presence in Lewiston by sharing the Forum's office. Why the need of yet another international development group? The key word for passage was 'Franco' and it was funded as an offering to the Franco community as a result of pressure brought by a highly visible politician.

By the year 2002 the Forum Francophone des Affaires was out of business and the Maine International Trade Commission was now sharing office space with the L&A Economic Growth Council. And close to a quarter of a million dollars had literally been wasted. Could this honestly be justified?

LEWISTON-AUBURN COLLEGE START-UP FUNDING

To have a University of Maine campus in Lewiston or not was a big question. On two occasions a referendum election was held in Lewiston. Both times, the voters soundly rejected the proposal. Why? What was the issue, and who was against establishing a university presence in the twin cities of Lewiston-Auburn? Yet the push continued and the issue centered on whose land a proposed campus should be situated. The initial cost was projected to be $1.1 million. After both referenda had failed, supporters proposed that legislation be introduced to promote the local college. It was not the idea of having a local campus but rather that the owners of Shelter Group, a low-income housing developer and manager and owners of the proposed sites, were to be the main beneficiaries.

Legislation was introduced with an accompanying fiscal note. However when it became apparent that there was not enough support at the State House to enact it, it was decided to try incorporating it into the budget document. But even in the Appropriations and Financial Affairs Committee the support was not evident. The reasoning was that since Lewiston was within thirty miles or so of other campuses, building yet another school would have eroded the financial resources affecting other campuses. The proponents were not deterred. Finally the Democrats on the committee were called to a caucus in the Senate chairman's office hoping that some support could get us out of this impasse…I say us because I was a member of that Committee. Clearly even the Democrats were not impressed by arguments for increasing the university budget since future added costs would have to be factored in. After a few moments, seeing an impasse, a member of the Committee left the room and within a few minutes the Speaker of the House, John L. Martin, with morning coattails flying, pushed the door open with Mr. Nadeau on his heels.

"Any progress?" demanded Martin.

"None," replied Chairman Mike Pearson.

"Okay, here's what you do," Martin said in his best take-charge tone. "Place an additional $3.1 million into the University budget, earmarked this way: $1.1 for Lewiston, and the rest allocated to the campuses of Farmington, Machias, Fort Kent and Southern Maine. None for Orono." Martin had deftly covered all the Districts of the Appropriation Committee members. They eagerly agreed. End of the impasse. Senator Pearson shook his head in disbelief. Lewiston's campus was finally funded for the first year. Once again, Speaker Martin had displayed his masterful approach to resolving problems while asserting his authority.

MAINE NATIONAL GUARD LICENSE PLATES

In 1975 legislation was introduced to allow members of the Maine National Guard to purchase special license plates for their cars. For a fee of $5 they could acknowledge being part of a group of men and women who undertake tasks in our state thereby saving scarce money for the taxpayer, as they are also ready when called to join our forces overseas during a time of emergency.

The House overwhelmingly endorsed the enactment of the bill, followed by approval in the Senate though by a smaller margin. After the Senate's approval it was sent to the Governor's desk for his signature. Unfortunately, Governor James Longley vetoed it as he felt it could be viewed as discriminatory to other groups who were not able to have their distinctive plates thus, in his eyes, creating a precedent.

During the ensuing debate the Representative from Gorham, Rodney Quinn, listened to the opponents' arguments and then rose from his seat to rebut the arguments against this bill. He addressed the issue of a precedent by saying that we already had precedent for unique or unusual plates and that denying the Guard their own is, in effect, clear discrimination. He then read into the record random names of plates that are legally in use in Maine, or at least at the time:

Foot, Foosie, Fosie, Goofy, Gootz, Guke, Boogie, Beep, Chink Chinh, Chunk, Doobie, Doodle, Doodie, Hokie, Hong, Honk, Honkey, Hooch, Hosana, Mousie, Twerp, Turkey, Turnip Snafu, Snuggy, Shnatch, Waddle, Weasel, Zak, Zeb, Zibble, Zig, Zilch, Unreal. He continued by saying that there are some that identity the U.S. Navy, Army, Air Force plus One-Eye, Mud-Pie, Big Head, Big-Boy, Hot-Dog while mentioning those that fit into another category, and fall in an interesting order: See-Me, Ask-Me, Try-It, Oh-Sam, Virgin, I-Dunno, Love-U, Y-Knot, Quick, Oops, At-Last, Did-It, Ow, No-Swet, I Fix-em, Repent. He had skillfully checkmated the precedent argument.

The House members overrode the veto 106-36 with more than the 2/3 vote needed. However, the Senate was not as accommodating with a vote of 16-15 with the majority favoring but not enough for a 2/3 vote of 23 and the bill therefore died.

At the next Session I co-sponsored the same measure and it met the same fate based on the same arguments and a similar vote. The Senate debate was more acrimonious with comments like "Next it will be Boy and Girl Scouts, the Mickey Mouse Fan Club." One Senator from Cumberland

County referred to the Guard as a "trivial organization" but he apologized at the next session.

Members of the National Guard had proposed this legislation but the opposition came from both Parties, mostly from the liberal wing of the Democratic Party, and was an indication of the anti-military feeling which exists in the legislative body in Augusta.

GOVERNMENT

STATE AUDITOR ELECTION

Maine is one of only a handful of States that select their Constitutional officers by vote of the Legislature, thus ensuring that the majority Party also controls these offices. The winners are generally Party activists, often defeated candidates with no previous experience since none is required. Proposed legislation has been introduced in the past that would mandate experience and training as an auditor or finance person such as a banking background, but this was always defeated.

Maine is also the only state that has its Attorney General selected by the Legislature. Prior to the start of the Legislative session, the two chambers meet in convention, and after the respective caucuses have nominated their candidate, a vote is taken by the entire membership. While it is expected that the majority Party's chosen one will prevail, sometimes there are hair-raising near misses due in part to the secret ballot used.

Such was the case in January 1977 when defeated congressional candidate Leighton Cooney was selected by the Democrats as their nominee for State Treasurer. Ninety votes were needed to win, the ballots were tabulated, and a look of disbelief came across Speaker Martin's face. Mr. Cooney had received 90, only one vote to spare. If all the Democrats had voted as expected for their candidate, Mr. Cooney would have had many more.

At the start of another biennial session in January 1979, the independence of some members surfaced once again. The incumbent State Treasurer lost his re-election bid to this plush state post. He lost to Republican Jerrold Speers who received 94 votes. Again, the Democrat caucus had the numerical advantage. What had happened? On the other hand, Rodney Quinn, a moderate Democrat, was elected as Secretary of State. Quinn received 92 votes, while his Republican opponent Linwood Palmer garnered 91 votes. It was clear that members were no longer blindly accepting the wishes of their leader.

The most interesting election for constitutional officer took place in the beginning of the 1977 session. The State Auditor, Rodney Scribner, resigned in order to accept an appointment in the federal government in Washington, DC. He was a fixture in state government having served in various posts as State Auditor, State Treasurer and State Comptroller. In 1979 he returned to Maine and was appointed Commissioner of the Department of Finance and Administration. A replacement was needed as a Democratic nominee for State Auditor. I was approached by a 14-year employee of the Department of Audit who indicated his interest in the vacated position. The Democratic leadership had already given their endorsement to a defeated House candidate, Representative Philip Ingegneri from Bangor. He was qualified by virtue of having been a U.S. Treasury auditor. The Democrat caucus voted to nominate Mr. Ingegneri over George Rainville, the state employee vying for the position. Mr. Ingegneri was assured of a job since once again, a Democrat majority would carry the day, and in view of the numbers, in all probability the other Party would not field a candidate. But today was different.

Mr. Rainville was a life-long Democrat and also a resident of my City of Lewiston. Ingegneri was considered by many, including Democrats, to be an extremely liberal legislator when he served, and it was hoped that a more moderate candidate would be selected. After the caucus vote, the leader of the minority Republican Party, Representative Linwood Palmer, approached me indicating that they would not cast one ballot for my Party's nominee as was the custom because they considered our nominee far too liberal. He inquired as to how many of my fellow Democrats would vote for Mr. Rainville if the Republicans placed his name in nomination. I was dumb-founded, but I nonetheless scurried around to get a feel of those whom I thought might consider such action. To my surprise several indicated that they would indeed support the career state employee. I must add that those legislators were also fellow Franco-Americans like George Rainville. Since he was also my constituent from Lewiston, I felt no qualms in supporting him. It might, however, be h... to pay.

"There are eight signed in blood," I reported to Palmer.

"Good," he said, "we'll nominate him."

Rainville, a slight man of few words, looked uncomfortable in an arena different from the environment of numbers and ledger sheets to which he was accustomed, but he walked about introducing himself. He was called into the office of the majority leader, Representative James Tierney who strongly urged him to withdraw his name, but was rebuffed by the straight-shooting candidate. Tierney was not about to give up and immediately hustled him into the Speaker's office where he was admonished: "Don't get involved." Again he refused, saying that too many legislators had gone to bat for him and he would not let them down.

A man of impeccable reputation for integrity and a man of total honesty and fairness, his meek deportment covered a strong determination to do what was right. It was a hectic day for this Lewiston resident.

The vote was carried out in the usual manner for election of a constitutional officer, with the membership marching down the middle aisle of the House chamber to drop their ballot in the box in front of the Speaker's rostrum. Speaker Martin had come down from behind the podium and stood at the box eyeing every ballot dropped. The number of votes needed to win: 90. When the tally was done, the results showed that Ingegneri had 79, and Rainville 96!

Stunned and angry at having been deprived of this plum appointment for the next four years, Tierney called me to the rear of the Chamber and said: "We've forgiven you for the Cohen endorsement, but we'll never forget this."

Subsequently the state's new auditor was re-elected to another 4-year term and he would acquit himself with competency and total integrity, but pressure kept building on him to leave and he eventually did.

I never regretted my support nor did he ever disappoint us.

COUNTY GOVERNMENT

County Government is an obsolete and costly third layer of governmental bureaucracy handed down from the reign of Charlemagne. County Government dates back many centuries – to the days of Emperor Charlemagne, the Great Frankish King, who ruled around 814. He controlled vast lands in what is now known as France, Germany and a great part of Western Europe. He needed help to control these large but sparsely populated lands and so he organized them into farm districts called *comtés* (counties) controlled by counts. The duties of the counts or administrators (now called Commissioners) were the following:

- To recruit troops
- To collect taxes, where they used sword and lance then, now they send an assessment bill to towns and cities subsequently paid by the property owners, many retired on fixed income
- To keep records

But these officials, Counts, couldn't be trusted. Some were known to keep some of these expropriated tax monies from those too scared to resist. And so in order to keep his Counts in line, Charlemagne appointed royal commissioners to report directly to him on the actions of his Counts. The concept of counties found its way to England, and during the Norman Conquest in 1066, William the Conqueror found an England made up of land divisions called Shires. He renamed those Shires Counties, and those counties became controlled by royal officers called Sheriffs. There were good ones and bad ones, like the Sheriff of Nottingham. Interestingly, Maine's first county was York, called Yorkshire then. But that was the 11th century. In the 17th and 18th centuries the concept of counties was transported with the colonists to North America where there were no strong centralized local governments.

During colonial times county government provided cohesion between towns far apart, but with today's highways, technology, and with law enforcement services provided by municipalities, the time has come to deal with the repeal of this duplicative system no longer needed in the 21st century. Past attempts to do so however have failed miserably.

One of its many liabilities is the negative impact it has on municipal costs. In some rural areas, such as Aroostook and Washington counties, there is still a need for consolidation of services under this umbrella called County Government. But to urban areas it becomes a costly burden that is once again borne by property taxpayers. Since County revenue is derived mainly on its assessment to Cities and Towns, there is nothing that can be

Thank You, Georgette

done to alleviate the cost burdens incurred. Municipalities in turn pass on these costs to their own source of revenue, the property tax. Most citizens have little or no benefit from county services. Those departments that are needed, for example Probate and Deeds, are generally self-sustaining through fees for services.

To create programs and government agencies is the easiest thing to do. To reduce or repeal them is next to impossible. I co-sponsored this measure to abolish County Government because we are talking of a medieval system that can no longer be justified. We are talking of a system that had increased my City of Lewiston's share of County Government support from approximately $485,000 in 1986 to $1.3 million in 1989 and $1,7million in year 2000. Totally out of whack! There were numerous views expressed increasingly by my constituents relative to County Government:

- It has outlived its usefulness
- It is a costly extra layer of bureaucracy
- It has a negative impact on our property taxes

These comments were written on the questionnaires returned to me from my district. The survey indicates that:

- Towns favored this bill by 58%, with 30% against, the rest undecided.
- Lewiston favored it by 62%, with 22% against, the rest undecided.

We hear that County Government serves a valuable purpose. Obviously the Register of Deeds and Probate, but together they are more than self-sufficient and could be maintained without cost to property taxpayers. Androscoggin County generated $365,000 in 2001 for both, so much so that monies could be returned to the local municipality since it would never cost that much to maintain these services.

Some provinces of Canada, i.e. Québec, have abolished their county form of government. What may have been needed in colonial days of 1689 is no longer viable or reasonable years later, for you see we have developed strong state and municipal government, governments which deal with jails, with law enforcement, with property taxes. And that triplication is an unfair and unbearable burden on our people, particularly for a system that has outlived its usefulness. There is no justification for allowing this galloping segment of governance to remain, for it merely places citizens on a collision course with financial self-destruction, with little accountability in return.

The bill to abolish County Government had been amended to allow each County to determine by vote whether they wanted to do away with this form of government. Most likely the urban counties would opt for leaving while the rural counties would elect to remain as they are now. This issue will re-appear in future sessions. Some day it may even happen.

COUNCIL ON AGING

A committee on Aging was initially set up in 1971 to serve as an advisory board to the Governor and the Department of Human Services, as well as to promote activities that meet the needs and addresses problems facing the elderly. It would also serve to organize a biennial Blaine House Conference on Aging where the elderly would be bused to the Augusta Civic Center to give input into suggestions and to testify before legislators on the needs that they would be told were essential to giving services. Also, federal dollars would be available.

The year 1973 saw a restructuring of elderly programs and the Committee was placed under the umbrella of the Bureau of Maine's Elderly. The budget of $250,000 for the biennium was for administrative costs only.

In 1991, in the dark days of a large budget shortfall, state employees were furloughed, and the Legislature, in order to preserve direct services for Mainers, eliminated several advisory boards and commissions, including the Committee on Aging. It was the feeling of the members of the Appropriations Committee and the State and Local Government Committee that the annual funding to maintain these boards would be better utilized toward direct services. Since then many attempts have been made to re-instate this phased-out Committee under a new name, the Council on Aging, but with the same language and $137,000 requested for the first year.

It should be stated that over the past thirty years, our Legislators have been responsive to the elderly segment of our population that has contributed much to our state through the years. They worked and paid their taxes, they served in the military during our wars and they did not beg for yet another council but much preferred such programs as low-costs drugs, and rent and tax refunds which were much more needed than what was proposed. It is hard to reconcile the urgency of creating another board when there are waiting lists of as many as seven hundred for home-based care.

We should not use the elderly for personal agendas. Did we really need more boards? To speak in behalf of our elderly population, there are presently the Bureau of Maine's Elderly, the Long-Term Steering Committee which advises the Governor and the Commissioner of Human Services, also a Long-Term Implementation Committee, not to forget AARP, the Maine Senior Citizens Council, and other advocacy groups. This should suffice.

Georgette B. Bérubé

The years 1999 and 2000 were also years of budget constraints, but regardless of the financial health of our state, a strong attempt was again made by a handful of individuals to create a new Council. House members approved it but the Senate defeated the proposal as unnecessary. Two lobbyists were constantly present around the Senate chamber until the last moment of the regular session hoping that somehow it could be saved. Elderly clients of services were asked to call those Senators who were reluctant to bring the proposal back to life. When the callers were asked if they would rather give up on some program for the elderly and use some of that money to create a Council, the answer was invariably: NO!

But lobbyists and advocates don't give up easily and this will be resurrected eventually. If there is so much loose change lying around, consideration should be given to those who are on waiting lists for services.

QUEBEC STATE VISIT

During a private visit to the City of Québec, I met the Chairman of the Conseil de Vie Française en Amérique, Monsignor Paul-Emile Gosselin. We tossed out ideas on ways that could be employed to build on all which links Maine and that Canadian Province, particularly in the areas of culture, education, economy and communications. At one point, he suggested that perhaps a state visit by the Governor of Maine would indeed attach greater importance to exchanges that could increase awareness of the many assets both governments possess. I was sold on the idea.

Upon my return I met with Governor Kenneth Curtis to discuss the offer supported by the Québec Prime Minister. The Governor enthusiastically agreed that he would participate in this visit. And so, after several visits by the chief of Protocol of the Québec Government, a hand-delivered invitation written by Prime Minister Robert Bourassa would welcome the Maine delegation for a two-day visit May 4th and 5th, 1972. The delegation would be composed of Governor Curtis, his cabinet, members of the press and Franco-American members of the Legislature.

Our flight took off from Bangor International Airport in a chartered Air Canada Viscount and in one hour we landed at the Québec Airport, l'Ancienne Lorette where we were greeted by Jean-Maurice Tremblay chief of Protocol, and the Deputy Prime Minister, Gérard D. Lévesque. After welcoming words we climbed into our assigned Provincial police cars for a motorcycle-led escort into the city to the Château Frontenac where we were staying. The ten-mile trip was an attention getter as we whizzed down Boulevard Laurier to the hotel with sirens blaring.

Meetings with our Québec hosts and counterparts were held during the two-day stay. At a state dinner that evening, the Governor endeared himself to our hosts when he opened his remarks by saying: "I did not have the good fortune to have been born a Franco-American, but I had the common sense to marry one." Applause. Laughter. Total success.

Before we departed for our trip home, the Prime Minister and Governor issued a communiqué touching on the areas of:

Education
- Student exchanges, particularly for those engaged in studies in public administration
- Exchange of professors and collaboration between research centers

Culture
- Exchange between the Portland Symphony Orchestra and the Québec Symphony Orchestra, art exhibits, films, books

Communications
- Québec assist in initiating a French radio station

Transportation
- Work on joint studies of mutual highway systems

Economy
- Expand exchanges of goods and jointly work to diminish diseases afflicting our forests, its habitat as well as obstacles regarding temporary laborers in the lumber industry

This raised the interest of the private sector and it was encouraging news to them. The following year, in 1973, the Quebecers came on a reciprocal visit led by Prime Minister Robert Bourassa. The warmth of our reception and Maine at its best went a long way to cement the relationship between our two governments. It kept the doors open to the dialogue which continues.

The creation of a Maine-Canadian Legislative Commission set up with a bill that I sponsored would facilitate contacts with the Government of Québec and serve as a liaison between Maine and Québec. It functioned as hoped until funding was cut during the budget crises of the early 1990s when some of its functions were transferred to the office of the Speaker. In my view $40,000 annual budget accomplished much of importance for the state.

A FAREWELL

Much has changed since I was first elected to the Legislature. In the year 1971, the House of Representatives had 15 women as opposed to 36 in 1999; the Senate had only one female Senator, Catherine 'Kitty" Carswell, a Democrat from Portland, who, when she spoke, held the attention of her colleagues and was highly respected in both Parties. She was a staunch Democrat with an open mind. By the time I left, women held leadership positions on both sides of the aisle, chaired committees, held major posts in government and no longer were simply brushed aside and delegated to collecting money for flowers or make coffee...or organize card parties as in 1970.

The biennial budget stood at $375 million in 1971, but by the year 1999, it had jumped to $4.5 billion with a $290 million surplus, which was promptly spent. This certainly impacted the budget down the road, and in 2003 was projected to be $5.3 billion. While it is risky to bank on future surpluses, which may or may not be there, the new expenditures created with these extra costs as well as the tax reduction of 1% in the sales tax must be taken into account in the next budget.

What has not changed, however, is the commitment and dedication most elected officials bring to the Capitol. For most, their loyalty is to their constituents, which is as it should be. It also explains why there are such divergent views on hunting laws, gun control, fisheries, and dairy products, all depending on who makes up your constituency.

Tempers may heat up in debate or for other reasons, yet let some illness or tragedy strike a member, irrespective of Party affiliation, the entire membership of the Senate and House stand together as one to bring solace and assistance to the stricken member. In 1995 I was quite ill. Their cards, phone calls and visits to the hospital and at my home were very heart-warming. Words such as "hurry back because during your absence they are on a spending spree" hastened my recovery. A blood drive was organized in my behalf at the State House and 162 units were collected. The Secretary of the Senate said: "I was happy to donate a pint of 'liberal' blood and it may affect your political views." My response was that I was pleased to receive any kind of political blood but that I had inquired from my surgeon if indeed it could make me a liberal. I was told that within a few weeks we renew our own blood supply. So I would still remain a moderate!!!

I was truly moved by my fellow Senators' kind gestures as well as those of lobbyists and the legislative staff. Upon my return, it was announced that each Senator would like to present me with a token of their respect

Georgette B. Bérubé

and happiness that I was on the mend. The 34 members, excluding myself, came one by one to my desk and presented me with a long-stemmed rose…34 red roses…they adorned my desk for several days reminding me that personal disagreements over issues seem so unimportant taken in the context of loyalty, friendship, life and death.

In the year 1996 term limits applied to me, and it was time to go. The following election I ran, was re-elected but chose not to run again in 2000. My parting words to the Senate were:

> *"Partir, c'est mourir un peu." (To leave is to die a little.)*
> *I leave this Chamber with fond memories. I leave with the satisfaction of having done what I promised to do when I ran and that was to represent my fellow-citizens with the dignity they deserve. And I leave with friendships made, some enduring. On the day of my last election I was apprehensive as usual, and I received flowers from my son with a card which simply said: 1 Timothy 4:7.*
> *I looked it up and I would like to leave you with the words I read:*
>
> > *I have fought the good fight*
> > *I have finished the race*
> > *I have kept the Faith*
>
> *Thank you all very much.*

POT POURRI

LUNCHEON CANCELED?

Most legislators are honest and dedicated. They represent their constituencies as best they can. Others serve for personal glory or as a stepping-stone to higher office. Some simply cannot tolerate the hard-working members and instead of lending support, criticize unfairly and try to disparage their colleagues even going so far as to scuttle initiatives meant to better serve the people of our state.

Such was the case when an out-of-state shoe company announced that it would locate in Auburn but that it needed assistance from the Department of Economic Development (DED). A noon luncheon meeting was set up at the request of Senator John Cleveland of Auburn, in order for the Lewiston-Auburn delegation to be informed and also meet with officials of the company as well as the Commissioner of DED. Shortly before noon as I was working at my desk I received a visit from an Auburn legislator who informed me that the meeting had been canceled. Surprised that I had not been told of the change, I said that I would call the Comfort Inn where the luncheon was to be held. She assured me that it was not necessary and left. Nonetheless I placed the call and was told that the meeting was being held as scheduled.

I hurried over arriving a few minutes late and was greeted at the door by Representative Susan Dore of Auburn and Senate Majority leader Nancy Clark.

"I'm so glad you're here," said Nancy. "No one has arrived other than John, Susan and me."

I explained that I also nearly had not come as I had been told that the meeting had been cancelled. Her look of disbelief followed by a wry smile said it all:

"I had heard that someone had tried to scuttle it," she said.

Upon our return to the State House, as John, Susan and myself sat in the second floor stately rotunda exchanging thoughts, the reporter from the Lewiston Daily Sun walked by.

"Gary, who told you that the meeting had been canceled?" queried Susan.

"I'll let you guess," was his smiling reply.

POLLING

We should not always believe poll results, for things are not always what they may appear to be. As an example, I was walking toward the elevator adjacent to the Senate chamber, and as I stepped into the car, the long arm of a lobbyist from the Christian Civic League held the elevator door for me. He had followed me from the chamber and asked if I would support another tax increase on alcoholic beverages, an increase the League supported. My response was clear: "absolutely not!" He turned to his assistant, who had a clipboard in hand: "Put her down as undecided," he said.

SENDING NOTES

Legislators are not allowed to leave their seat in order to speak with another member at his or her desk during a session. If they must talk to a colleague, they will send a note by one of the pages asking to meet in the rear of the House or Senate chamber. Notes can deal with the legislation being debated, casual comments, or even a game of tic tac toe if the debate is long and boring. I still have some of those notes, some just for conversation, others asking for a vote on a particular issue. I have gleaned a few:

The following note from the then Speaker, David Kennedy, was trying to change my vote against a gasoline tax increase:

> *"Why! Why! We gave you a bridge-it needs approaches, etc., etc. My country roads need repairs. PLEASE."*

I held firm.

On a Bill dealing with the Equal Rights Amendment (ERA), I received the following note from the sponsor after I had debated the issue. My reason for opposing it at the time was that women's protective labor laws would be repealed. There was much opposition including the AFL/CIO. The next year when it was re-introduced, I supported it because by then the Department of Labor was no longer enforcing these laws. The note said:

> *"Georgette, You're dead wrong-but deadly. I still love you."*
> *Kathy*

One man was being rather long-winded in expressing his reasons for supporting a measure before us. The note I received said:

> *"If you believe as he does, you better send him a note and tell him it's too long. He's damaging your cause. If you are against him, then let him talk."* Bob

While I served as Speaker Pro-Tem, a sampling of notes read:

> *"Madam Speaker, GOOD JOB! The gang is proud!!!* Angela
> *"Watch out for your blood pressure."* Tony
> *"I can see why he put you up there! He (the Speaker then) would have folded under the pressure."* Jim
> *"Political courage is suicide. Right on!"* Dot

After my remarks in support of a Power Authority of Maine

> *"Congratulations. You gave a fine presentation and you have the support of this grey-haired old Republican"* Harold

Georgette B. Bérubé

On another member serving as Speaker Pro-tem:

"See what a goddam hypocrite this bastard is. He knows the bilingual Bill is coming up. I know that's his reason for being up there." 'Mr. D'

After a heated debate on a spending bill, I got the following note:

"Go get 'em. Tiger" Dick

Of all the notes I received over the years, I treasure a short one from a 6-year-old boy who was a page for that day:

"Madam, I hope your done by 5 because I leaving for my hockey." Claude

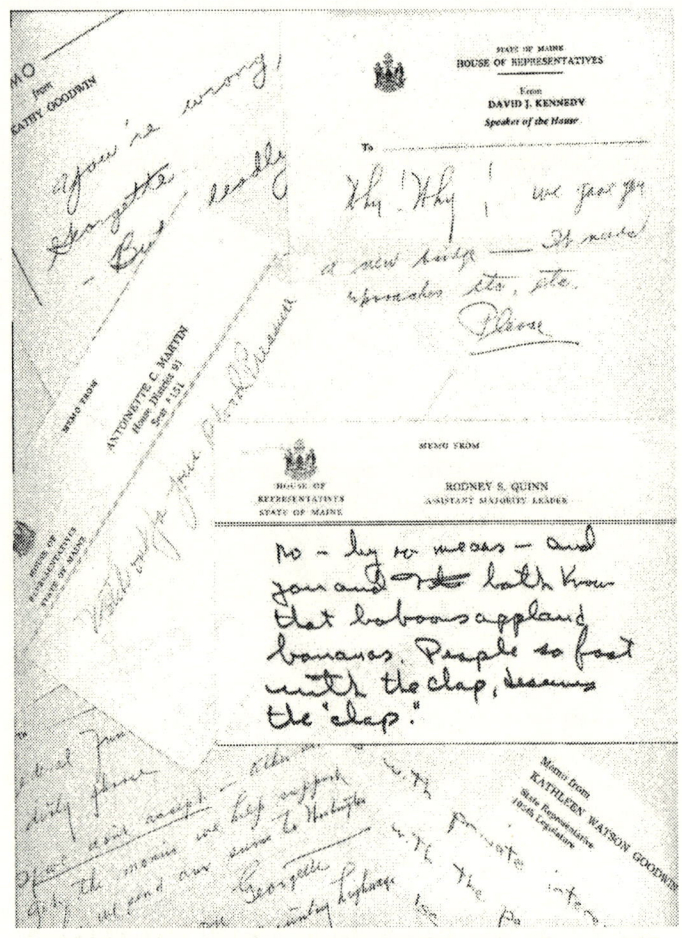

"It's unfortunate that the notes legislators send to each other often do not find themselves in archives; we might learn more about the legislation and the legislators themselves."]

CONDOMS DEBATED

The bill being debated would have removed the need of a license to sell (prophylactic) rubber goods. The debate became long and repetitive. The lady from Newcastle, Representative Charlotte Byers, rose from her seat and said: "I feel that we must defend this bill as a good bill. It came out of Committee and everybody thought that it should pass. Without going into it in great detail and without stretching it out of proportion." It took a while before order was restored.

ANIMALS IN STORES

The legislation before the House was "An Act to Prohibit Bringing Animals into Food Stores and Restaurants." The gentleman representing the Town of Oakland, upon being recognized by the Speaker quickly got to his feet. Nearly bald, glasses hanging loosely on his nose, short of physical stature with a serious expression on his face, so totally wrapped up into his remarks that he did not realize the humor of his words, he stood at his microphone balancing himself on his toes and proceeded to explain the reason for supporting this measure:

This Bill gives the right for all blind people to enter with their dog. It also allows the man who owns it to leave a dog there to protect it. There is nothing wrong with that. Maybe some of you people have been into a store and I saw a dog in there, and there was sugar there. I know what the dog did on the sugar and I saw the young lady buy the sugar.

By then the entire Chamber was grinning and laughing. He continued, unaware of his audience's reaction and oblivious to his surroundings:

Now, I didn't call this very good. I also went into Zayre's in Waterville and I had on a brand new pair of shoes and I felt something slippery. Now I am not going to explain what it was because I cannot here on the floor, but I think you have all good education to know what I am talking about.

At this point the Speaker could not contain himself any longer and had joined the laughter. The Representative continued

The lady who had the big elephant of a dog who messed my shoe all up, she just said "that poor dog couldn't hold it any longer." They went out and they got a poor little girl who worked there, to come in with napkins and wash it up. She worked there, she had to be a slave. I think the woman who had the dog should have done it. I didn't ask her to wash it off my shoes, but it didn't smell very good even when I got in the car. This Bill has nothing to do with eliminating dogs of blind people. It has nothing to do at all with the man who owns the store. If you folks run through it, I don't have too many shoes, and I hope that this won't happen to you.

By then the entire Chamber was roaring with laughter and Speaker Martin made no effort to gavel to order. Representative Jalbert couldn't resist getting up and remarking: "I know that everybody is going to agree with me when I say that the gentleman from Oakland, Mr. Brawn, is priceless."

RANDOM THOUGHTS

"Long before a woman served as a Speaker of the House in her own right, I was honored by being one of the first women to serve as Speaker Pro Tempore. Wielding the gavel even for a short time seemed unthinkable for a young girl during the Great Depression."]

OVERVIEW

I believe in the maxim "Do it because it is right, not because someone is watching." Soon I would learn that members are not supposed to act independently from leaders. But I also learned that standing up for your beliefs and placing faith in the citizens are far more rewarding. My philosophy was to level with the voters, keep an open mind and change views if it was justifiable to do so. During my 26 legislative years a few of the die-hard PARTY COMES FIRST belief were not tolerant of those who disagreed with them, but the leadership was generally helpful to me.

There is a French saying: *"Plus ça change, plus c'est la même chose."* (the more things change, the more they're the same.) Issues of concern in the 1970s re-surfaced in the 1990s, and in the first year of the 21st century, concerns with taxes, elderly issues, child care, health insurance were in the forefront, not to mention the old chestnuts which did not get passed in previous years and re-surfaced annually.

While tax revenues are needed to provide services, the Legislature must also address the people's ability to pay those same taxes. While the burden of a property tax has been eased somewhat with the State Tax and Rent Refund program, nonetheless it remains a regressive source of municipal revenue.

As advocates of various causes make more demands, we find that programs started with a modest appropriation generate into those with costly funding. As an example, the Business Equipment Tax Re-Imbursement (BETR) program was initiated in 1997 with start-up funding of $4.7 million and quickly rose two years later to $48 million. Once they are started it is most difficult, next to impossible, to stem the growth of programs, let alone doing away with them. And so, rather than reduce the funding, taxes remain the only way to maintain this *largesse* of government. Considered annually to fill the need for extra money is allowing the municipal governments to levy a local sales or income tax to be shared with the state. The bait? To say that property taxes will be reduced. What is meant is that local spending will continue to increase, but with an additional option, the rate of increase will be stemmed.

Continuously, local governments speaking through the Maine Municipal Association are hoping for removal of exemptions from the sales tax. It is estimated that if all goods and services were no longer exempt, that some $ 700million would be available to spend on new programs taken from wish lists. Frightening thought.

LEADERSHIP

It has been said that "Leadership is an executive ability: deciding quickly and getting someone else to do the work." Leadership is necessary if it is to be used to see to the general well being of a community. It is not so good when it is self-serving. Leadership implies initiative and willingness to work and to accept consequences. Self-confidence, "the buck stops here," these are all ingredients needed for leadership.

Others recognize certain qualities in an individual which allow them to follow a leader who can pave the way. What determines this ability? Maybe some have a more engaging smile, they may campaign harder than others and this may indicate drive, or maybe they are taller. I recall an opponent who once told me that it's usually tall people who succeed in getting elected or in being leaders. He named Abraham Lincoln, Senator Muskie...and as I looked up to his 5'11" frame from my 5'3" I said, "and Napoléon Bonaparte, George Washington."

After being elected, the hard part is in trying to achieve success and meet goals while keeping peace with everyone. But not everyone aspires to be a manager or a company president or a school principal...some merely want to do their job and be given direction and guidance and, yes, even follow.

I once read in a magazine that when a girl applies at an eastern woman's college a questionnaire is sent to her parents. A father who was filling out the questions came to this one: "Is she a leader?" He hesitated, then wrote: "I am not sure about this, but I know she is an excellent follower." A few days later he received this letter from the President of the College: "As the Freshman group next fall is to contain several hundred leaders, we congratulate ourselves that your daughter will also be a member of the class. We shall thus be assured of one good follower."

Some seek involvement for opportunistic endeavors: power to achieve wealth at the expense of others. Power and wealth are tremendous motivators and yet oftentimes they leave destruction that causes followers to be disillusioned. This breeds contempt. Unless it is motivated by a cause, the reign of a strong-arm leader is generally short-lived. We need leaders who will attract others to work for the common good. We need "heroes, not zeros" or users of the system. While we live in an age of selfishness and cynicism, nonetheless we also live in an exciting time and we can handle the challenge. We need well-defined goals and the desire to work toward achieving them.

Whether one agrees with him or not, John L. Martin stands out as a leader. His knowledge of the legislative process, his charisma coupled with self-assuredness have led him to be a capable and successful leader which I expect he will continue to be.

As Françoise Giroud, the French author and Minister in the French cabinet wrote in '*La Comédie du Pouvoir* " (The Comedy of Power): "The state must serve. We legislators must neither use it for our benefit nor enslave others with that power."

FOLLOW THE LEADER

It is always easier to agree with the leaders of one's Party…no hassles, rewards with perks (trips, conferences, top Committee assignments). My own idea of loyalty was not necessarily to be 100% in agreement, but when appropriate to express my reasons for support or opposition of an issue. I did so directly with the leaders and also in caucus, and hoped other arguments might be considered. After witnessing some members constantly voting with the leaders' light on the electronic boards, I often thought that enormous cost savings could be achieved by simply having robots sit in the Legislative chambers and allow them to press the voting buttons on cue.

TERM LIMITS

While elective service can at times be demanding, the hard work translates into enacting laws designed to make life a little bit better for our fellow citizens. The downside is that it is more and more difficult to find people who want to seek public office. With term limits in place, there are more openings for those who might be interested in serving. With good government comes frank and open discussion from different viewpoints, for this fundamental right to free expression assures the survival of our democracy.

It is doubtful that the Legislature would have voted itself into term limits. Four terms (eight years) was not an acceptable proposition for those elected officials who crave the power to which they may have become accustomed. The citizens of Maine, and without much persuasion I might add, willingly contributed to the 88,000 plus signatures gathered to force a referendum which was subsequently approved by the voters. Some elected officials would have liked to cling to power, going so far as to take the matter to court with the purpose of usurping peoples' wishes expressed loud and clear by passage of the referendum.

Term limits do not pose a bleak outcome to our democracy. First, a House or Senate member after his/her eight years (if re-elected) can run for the other chamber for yet another four terms. We saw it in the 2002 election. Secondly, if they still wish to seek re-election to their current seat, taking a two-year sabbatical away from the State House will not harm the citizens. In 1994 sixteen states had voted in favor of term limits with more states since then. My Party was opposed to term limits, but I felt that although some good hard-working legislators might be forced out, it was the only way to take away the power that some had accumulated, either through leadership positions or committee chairmanships.

No seat is a given, yet some legislators expressed the true reason for opposing this limit: "this seat is mine." Well, it is not. Everyone has a chance to make a run for office. If competent candidates are elected, this will bring in fresh ideas and new energy. It is interesting to note that some first-timers who ran for office because their own legislator was termed out, now espouse, and very vocally, that term limits are bad for us.

One valid argument against term limits is that there is a loss of historical perspective as well as institutional knowledge. Staff and bureau heads would also have a greater say in drafting legislation since the new inexperienced newcomers would rely on them. Lobbyists would also play a part in the "education" of the freshmen. But that is already done now even to seasoned legislators.

There is however one flaw and that is that the Legislature can undo the citizens' vote by repealing this law. We will hear all the arguments for doing away with term limits, but we will not hear that since its implementation the state has continued to survive. The long-reigning King of France, Louis X1V is credited with the following remark: *"L'Etat c'est moi, et après moi, le déluge."* (I am the State, and after me, the deluge). Though he fancied himself as being indispensable, France survived without him and has done so to this day. With or without its present legislators, Maine will continue to exist with new ideas, with new faces, and with new energy.

People evolve and change; their philosophy also changes. I found through these years that the Democratic Party was not the same as the one in which I grew up. Taking over its direction is an elitist element, which is reflected in the legislation that is enacted or attempted to be. The conservative or moderate Democrat no longer appears to have a place in this great Party that did much for workingmen and women. They were not anti-business but sought a fair return for the workers who contributed so much to the success of commercial and industrial enterprises. Those who have taken over do not try to include the feeling of constituents and so we see whole communities with a majority thinking one way, yet not having a single vote from their legislative delegation to reflect their thinking. If such is the case, why are these people elected? Very simply: they spout the rhetoric that they believe will ingratiate them to a constituency, they send mailings prepared by staff and have a ready-made answer to explain their vote. During campaigns we hear most of them say that they "will fight for you." If they all "fight" in Augusta, is there any time left to really study the impact that proposed laws will have on our communities and entire state? Both Parties suffer from the same ailment: they have allowed the ultra left and ultra right to inflict their philosophy on the Parties…and when most of our citizenry is centrist.

Term limits should not be feared.

SPENDING / TAXES

If elected officials were as cautious with spending tax dollars as they are with their own funds, over-spending would decrease, especially if the low priority expenditures were curtailed until deficits are eliminated. Pork-barrel give-aways, which are often slipped into the budget document or included in a popular bond issue, contribute to shortfalls. This last example carries the risk of defeating a perfectly-good bond issue by including unrelated pork which too often does nothing for the common good. The questions arise: should it be funded with an increase of a broad-based tax? Should it be curtailed?

There is concern among Mainers that many sales tax exemptions will be removed and the sales tax charged on services as well. There is a group favoring taxing every item, including food, which would bring in an additional $700 million. The bait being offered is that the sales tax rate of 5% could be reduced. But there is no guarantee. Mention is also made that new revenues could also be dedicated to education with a possible reduction in property tax growth. But there is no guarantee. The citizens of our state must not lose control of their state budget and how it is spent. The careful use of surpluses can do much good but it must be continuously scrutinized.

Concern has also been expressed for a proposal advanced by the Maine Municipal Association and several social services and activist groups to create the option of a local sales and income tax. With these new millions streaming into government coffers, we can only imagine the temptation to spend these newfound dollars. One senator, as we discussed the tax issue, was practically salivating thinking of this infusion of money.

Carefully looking into duplicative programs, plus considering the use of surpluses for renovating state-owned buildings and schools would save the interest costs of borrowing when there are surpluses. $80 million budgeted for principal and interest add greatly to the expense budget. With a state bonded indebtedness of approximately $500 million, we must be careful in passing bonds and sending them to the voters. Unless we address these issues, the shortfall hole will get deeper and deeper. As bond referenda are accepted, the cost of interest goes up, and it is projected that in the next budget repaying of principal and interest will rise to over $101 million in 2003, and still proposals are made and generally accepted.

REMARKS ON KEY ISSUES

POWER AUTHORITY OF MAINE, 5/6/91

Ladies and Gentlemen of the House:

As a signer of the Minority Report, and signing it strictly on the merit of the bill, I think that this deserves more than just an "ought to pass" vote on my part. I wish that I could muster all the eloquence heard here so many times so that I could convincingly state my reasons for supporting this measure.

We have seen the progress generated in other areas brought about by hydroelectric plants. I have seen this progress in our country and especially with our neighbors to the North. Here is an idea that can bring concrete economic improvement by offering cheaper industrial electric rates. Our people deserve a break when it comes to better paying jobs.

If this shows only half the progress seen elsewhere it will have been worthwhile. The State of Maine deserves also a chance finally to be brought into the 70s. We certainly need help on this score for we only have to look at the take home pay in the past and present. I discount the argument that a hydro-electric plant such as this envisions would create pollution problems, for I have seen some mighty clean rivers in the shadow of these generating plants and accompanying industry on the north shore of the St. Lawrence.

And how can we forget the consumer? The average cost per kilowatt-hour for residential use in Maine has been 2.75 as compared to 1.9 in Québec. Commercial and industrial sales, 1.3 per kilowatt-hour as compared to 0.7. This disparity has continued since the advent of hydroelectric complexes in that Province. The same has held true in other areas in our country. Now isn't it about time that the consumer be given a break? The average home use is a whopping $15.00 or more per month! And in a state which has swift rivers at its doorsteps!

We have, through various pieces of legislation, looked after the welfare of the moose and the fish, we have apple-polished the tourist for three months of the year, and yet we take for granted, but forget, the needs and the hopes of our people who must live and work for 52 weeks a year. Here is an opportunity to show our constituents that our state will finally take a giant step forward. We, the people of Maine, will benefit directly and indirectly from the profits derived from a public power authority.

When I ran for this Legislature I said my reasons for doing so were that I wanted to represent the City whose citizens and I share the same goals and the same ideals. They want some new hope, and I want some purpose in life. All of us are here to represent the people back home. And I stress represent. How can we turn our back on them once we're here? I've heard say many times that we believe in competitive business for this helps the consumer who is always the one to pay the bill. Let's give Maine a boost. Let's create our own Power Authority of Maine. This is the type of legislation which transcends all Party affiliation for the voter is our true employer: not Party, not private interest groups. Let us vote favorably on this bill.

HUMAN RIGHTS BILL (GAY RIGHTS) 3/28/91 SENATE CHAMBER

Many people have called or written to me expressing their views on this issue. All, irrespective of their philosophy, took time to do so and I as a Senator, want to listen to all sides and then seek advice and information in order to make a just decision on such an important bill.

Although I have been supportive of this proposal in the past, I harbored doubts such as that of proprietary rights. I am satisfied that the so-called 'Mrs. M Murphy's Law' will exempt those landlords/ladies residing in their own apartment buildings.

Arguments which impressed me:

A) Maine Medical Association endorsed this bill in order to facilitate treatment of HIV-infected persons without threat of retribution or shame if they come forward.

While the cases of infection have stabilized for the Gay community, statistics indicate an ever-increasing rate of HIV cases among the heterosexual. Many in this last group will not seek medical services terrified at being labeled "Gay." By the way, an employer cannot discriminate against an AIDS victim, yet can summarily dismiss a long-time competent employee based on the only fact that he/she may be Gay.

B) A chief of police said that this law is needed because while law enforcement officers must and do protect people and property, they cannot pursue cases judicially as victims refuse to come forward to press charges.

In my view, it's wrong when abused people cannot bring action against a perpetrator because they can't be themselves in this state – in this day and age – and fear job dismissal.

You know, gays are being painted as flaunting their homosexuality. I would counter that there are exhibitionists on both sides. But those few numbers are not indicative of the majority. Most people, whether homosexual or heterosexual, conduct themselves publicly in a responsible manner. This bill does not approve nor encourage irresponsible behavior.

Violence and sexual abuse against women and children are daily news items we're all familiar with – perpetrated mostly by heterosexual males. So the fear of lawlessness on the part of gays is an unjustified fear. Violence and sex crimes are not indicative of nor pertinent to a particular lifestyle.

During the Depression, we lived under Prohibition, but people found ways to distill and illegally import alcohol; resulting in deaths because of inferior products. We now have legalized alcoholic beverages, and though legal, it is being abused – yet the very people who misuse it are not fired from their jobs.

Extending rights in housing, employment, credit, public lodging to Gays/Lesbians will not invite more homosexuality – not any more than giving rights to atheists among believers in the Almighty.

Actions of pot smokers may be illegal acts but they are not evicted from their home or discharged from work. Civil Rights should not be denied to those who might have a relationship with another person of the same sex.

Taken in the context of University Presidents who squandered defense contract dollars on personal use – compared to public officials who lie, who live luxuriously while causing the loss of billions of dollars in Savings and Loans, of husbands who sexually abuse wives and daughters, taken in these contexts, I assure you that danger to our society from those who engage in a caring, loving, respectful relationship between two people wishing to share a life with one another, is indeed non-existent.

Passage of this legislation will not mean that we are giving our imprimatur to a personal lifestyle. But it will be seen as a forward step toward a more tolerant society. It is an issue of tolerance and human rights. It will not entirely prevent prejudices and biases toward those who are viewed as "acting differently from what societal mores are viewed as being the right ones." But it will be a step toward education and away from stigmatization. I am not known as a flaming liberal, but this is just right.

To those whose letters and words have undoubtedly sincerely expressed their Biblical beliefs, I would say that the Christian world this week-end is celebrating its greatest feast of renewal and optimism…it commemorates a God/Man who gave His life so that the sins of others might be forgiven – who said "that he who is without sin should cast the first stone"…who said that "the great and first commandment is to Love the Lord"…and who said that the second is like it, "you shall love your neighbor, for on those two depend all laws." The Roman Catholic Diocese has written that it is as a person that one has the right to protection against discrimination, and that does not necessarily mean condoning a personal lifestyle.

A young professional woman placed it all in perspective for me. Educated, intelligent, reasoned, and who had admitted having formed a relationship with another woman, she allayed any fear I might have had. She looked like we would want our daughter to be – she could also be our daughter. And as she prepared to leave, she said that she had not divulged to her mother as yet what she had told me because she was scared of her reaction. My response was that if it were my daughter who admitted to a relationship which might be different from the accepted norm, I would hold her and tell her I love her. Her mother would do the same.

This is a fair bill and I feel very comfortable in supporting it.

ABORTION, HOUSE CHAMBER
5/19/71

As legislators, our personal and moral convictions should never be forced on others as we have a duty to all of our constituents, but we must look at the issue and the merit of a bill.

Now, there is a freedom of choice...to conceive or not, and I believe that with freedom we must equate the word responsibility. We have heard countless arguments between the theological and the biological reasons for keeping or destroying human life, but if the human is not subservient to the biological, therefore the conduct to adopt as far as concerns human life cannot be dictated by criteria which are strictly scientific or political. The State of Maine further recognized the existence of the unborn young of animals and allows this as goods in a sale: the unborn young of humans deserve as much protection.

I may not have received as many letters as some, but I did get 96 pertaining to this issue, only three of which favored such legislation... clearly a large majority do not want liberalized abortion laws. While it may be true that there was a rash of letters written with much the same format, we must also bear in mind that so many of us cannot find the sophisticated words necessary to express our feelings and our concern, and consequently we look for the direction which will pave the way to our being heard. But the fact remains that people, just people, took the time to take pen in hand and write to their legislators. We should respect their wishes and remember that we serve at their pleasure. Out of the several reasons advanced for changing the present law, one of the most revealing is given by an insurance company which gives as its reason for supporting abortion bills that it is cheaper for them to pay for an abortion than for a four or five day hospital confinement for childbirth. Is this how we have come to measure social progress?

I cannot subscribe to this theory for I believe that material and cultural well-being can be achieved through the sharing of our great wealth, which in turn can be brought about by increased job opportunities, education, pride and respect in ourselves and our fellow-man...not by leading our generation into a faceless and soulless society.

I shall vote against this bill.

EQUAL RIGHTS AMENDMENT, HOUSE CHAMBER 2/27/73

The easiest thing for me today would have been to sit back, to avoid taking a public stand, and cast my vote with a vocal minority…but since this issue is one which would affect my children and my children's children, in conscience I must rise to explain why I shall oppose the Amendment. I am speaking as a wife, as a mother, as a worker, and as a teacher of my children of the respect of the rights of others and the respective responsibilities of each of which they will encounter during their adult lives. These are the rights and roles I wish to retain, but today I must also act as a legislator representing my city, and I am now sure that my vote will be a reflection of their concern and their ideals.

What is equality? Voltaire said, "They who say all men are equal speak an undoubted truth, if they mean that all men have an equal right to liberty, to their property, and to their protection of the laws, but they are mistaken if they think men are equal in their stations and employment since they are not so by their talents."

We are told that ratification of this amendment will assure equality to all women in the field of employment, in salary scales, in the military (although we should not fear this at the moment since the draft is no longer in use) and while it may be true that the protective labor laws for women are no longer being enforced, I could say that by the same token women would have to accept a job in a plant that she would not have requested. I might also say that in the case of wage differentials that the Equal Pay Act of 1963, Title VII of the Civil Rights Act of 1964 can be used to equalize and rectify injustices as was recently ordered upon American Telephone & Telegraph in the sum of $38 million. You know, some of we women have complained for years that men are solely responsible for women being held back. Certainly, they may have contributed to this, but we must take a hard look…some of us must work twice as hard as a man to get where we are…example, this very hall; however, oftentimes we must prove our competence not to men but to other women. We seem to perpetuate the prejudices against ourselves. We do not have faith in ourselves. Well, I do. I have faith in our Civil Rights Laws which extend to all people rights and justice and implements legislation to rule on violations when proven. In this very Chamber at the last special session we ordered the State University to equalize salaries of women professors in order to bring them to the level of the male educators.

Georgette B. Bérubé

The solution to so many of the problems of our age cannot be resolved by leading us to a faceless conformity. It is well for those who sit comfortable at the country clubs or speak from behind the protective economic shield of a comfortable profession, but whatever their reasons may be: animosity, blind following, cynicism, the feeling that it's the thing to do, these are not reflective of the wishes and needs of the women of this nation.

Recently I attended a meeting which had to do with presenting a program and project to a group representative of the people of Maine, and to find the best way of making it acceptable throughout the State. At one point someone said: "Perhaps we have been using the wrong approach, maybe we've been pushing vanilla when in reality the public wants strawberry." I agree, for when I went to school they taught me that Christopher Columbus had discovered American when in reality I knew better.

Perhaps we are trying to force a change which is not wanted. Of course we all want equal opportunity and that is why we have Title VII of the Civil Rights Act of '64, we have the Equal Pay Act of '63, the Equal Opportunities Act of '72. These are being implemented with the Equal Employment Opportunities Commission.

I have read with great interest the Briefs of the American Labors' Organizations relative to the status of working women in the field of employment, the military, and the home. Professor Paul Freund of the Harvard Law School states "this proposed amendment attempts to impose a single standard of sameness on the position of the sexes in all the multifarious roles regulated by law: marital support, parental obligations, social security, industrial employment, activities in public schools, and military service."

We have read and heard that some legislators would support this bill because they are gubernatorial candidates; others have made flippant statements while being fence sitters waiting for the tide to draw them in. Some admit that they oppose this legislation but that since they have committed themselves to certain organizations they must abide by their commitment. I cannot justify these reasons. We could understand agreements to support certain issues; the welfare of the moose and the fish, maybe even the hunter, even Mr. So and So's beehives...but never on an issue which on the surface is made to appear so simple and yet will affect the lives of so many people and will take away from them their duties and responsibilities toward their families. If this happens, someday we will have become a people with no identity. We will have been led in blind delusion into Huxley's Brave New World. We will have become a faceless and soulless society

DEMOCRATIC STATE CONVENTION 1982

Madam Chairman, Distinguished Platform Guests, Fellow Delegates, and friends:

We have come here this weekend to participate in what many may call meaningless ballyhoo and empty rhetoric. Yet the right of political Party association – the right to assemble freely here in convention – is as inalienable as the right to individual liberty.

If our political Party system and our politicians have fallen into low public esteem, it is because of lack of participation on the part of too many. A famous Southern conservative said that if men and women of capacity refuse to take part in politics, they condemn themselves as well as the people, to the punishment of living under bad government. A well-known black radical said that if you're not part of the solution, you're part of the problem. Both were right.

I believe that those of us here today are part of the solution. It has been said that applause, mingled with boos and hisses, is about all the average voter is able or willing to contribute to public life. I hope that those of us present in this hall today will contribute much more.

The years ahead will demand much more of each of us than have the years past. But let us not be afraid – together we can work to resolve our problems for the common good. It won't be an easy task in this age of selfishness, cynicism, and new Federalism, but it can be an exciting challenge – and I welcome it.

However, we in the Democratic Party must pull together and not apart. We must concentrate on those things that unite us and not on those that divide us. The Democratic Party is the product of men and women of vision who understood the tide of their times. They formed a Party that brought imagination, energy, and innovation to the nation and later to Maine. But above all, they form a Party of compassion – a Party of the truly needy and not a Party of the truly greedy.

We are a Party which is big enough and open enough for many people of divergent views: for the conservative and for the liberal, for the small businessman and woman and the mill worker, for the young and the old. Even though we may differ, we share the same concerns.

During the twelve years in which I have had the privilege of serving in the Maine House of Representatives, I have learned that if we will only listen to the people we can begin to address their problems. If we will but resolve our differences and dedicate ourselves to a common purpose, we

Georgette B. Bérubé

can then begin to work together toward easing our burdens and reach for the common good.

We must respect everyone whether they be the welfare mother or the wealthy Party contributor. For the most part, our Party is not made up of those who can go to the $1000-a-plate dinners or eat on quarter-of-a-million dollar china. It is made up of men and women who are simply trying to put food on the table for their families and who resent those who can eat caviar and then pretend that ketchup is a vegetable.

In these troubled times we must demand much of ourselves and of our elected officials. Politics cannot continue to be the only profession for which no preparation is thought necessary. We deserve – and we must demand – the best. Politicians rarely change their basic philosophy after they are elected. The candidate who does not understand the problems of his or her fellow citizens before the election will not be able to find the solutions after the election. We must demand strong leadership, moral integrity, political courage and vision.

- The Vision of a Maine which cares as much about its poor, its elderly, its disabled and its working men and women as it does about its wealthy corporations
- The Vision of a Maine which provides incentives to local small businesses instead of hand-outs to large out-of-state conglomerate
- The Vision of a Maine which provides tax equity to all citizens – where words such as "Safe Harbor " will continue to mean Camden or Rockport and not a rip-off for the rich
- The Vision of a Maine which will provide opportunities for higher education for all our young people despite the attempts of the Reagan Administration to undermine the very foundation of a free society – an education and informed citizenry.
- The Vision of a Maine which will be a place where our older citizens can retire and live with dignity and self-respect.
- The Vision of a Maine whose government will utilize the talents and resources of more than half its population – its women – where a female department head or judge will be more than merely a token.
- The Vision of a Maine whose people will elect a woman as their Governor.
- And finally, the Vision of a Maine which is nuclear free.

I am convinced that the continued existence of Maine Yankee represents a far more serious hazard than the economic impact of its closing. We in

Maine are blessed with common sense and good old-fashioned ingenuity. Through conservation, small-scale hydro-electricity such as produced by the Brunswick-Topsham Hydro we can and we will not mortgage the future of generations to come. Since Maine Yankee's inception, our electric bills have continued to skyrocket. How long must Maine consumers continue to subsidize utility mismanagement and boondoggle out-of-state investments?

One of Maine's most precious resources is her beautiful coast. If there were an accident at Maine Yankee, we couldn't give away our shore property. Part of the lifeblood of the Maine economy is our fishing industry – but who would buy Maine lobsters, shrimp, or scallops after a nuclear accident? And what about tourism? Who among you would take your family to Three-Mile Island for a vacation?

This earth does not belong just to us, and we have no right to leave it contaminated by carcinogenic poisons some of which remain toxic for hundreds of thousands of years. We must not view the environment as something we inherited from our ancestors, but rather as something we have borrowed from our children.

I recall a few years ago the Archbishop of Montreal, Cardinal Leger, announcing in church one Sunday that he was leaving all the material comforts of his Office to go to Africa to oversee a leper colony. He said: "If I say to you 'Go to Africa and take on this missionary work, only one or two might volunteer, but if I say instead – 'I am going, will you join me?' – maybe fifty or one hundred will come."

And so on this sunny May afternoon, I ask that you join with me in charting a New Direction for Maine. As John Kennedy once said, "Our task is not to fix the blame for the past, but to fix the course for the future." So let this be not the 'winter of our discontent' but rather the spring of our hope. I would like to leave you with this thought from Chaplain Hale:

> *I am only one, but I am one.*
> *I can't do everything, but I can do something.*
> *And what I can do, that I ought to do*
> *And what I ought to do, then by the grace of God I will do.*

ABOUT THE AUTHOR

Georgette Berube is a lifelong resident of Maine. From lessons during the Great Depression, World War II, and decades in her family's retail business, she became involved in politics in 1970, retiring thirty years later. Serving in both the Maine House and Senate, she has more state legislative service than another other woman in Maine's history. In 1982, she was a candidate for Governor of Maine. For many years she hosted a French radio show in central Maine and served on the Finance Council of the Catholic Diocese of Maine.

Printed in the United States
40211LVS00004B/68